100 VIGNETTES FOR IMPROVING TRIAL EVIDENCE SKILLS
Making and Meeting Objections

100 VIGNETTES FOR IMPROVING TRIAL EVIDENCE SKILLS
Making and Meeting Objections

ANTHONY J. BOCCHINO
JoANNE A. EPPS
DAVID A. SONENSHEIN

THE NATIONAL INSTITUTE FOR TRIAL ADVOCACy

Cover design by Jude Phillips

Bocchino, Anthony J., JoAnne A. Epps, and David A. Sonenshein, 100 *Vignettes for Improving Trial Skills* (NITA, 2005)

FBA0888
5/05   5/07

CONTENTS BY TOPIC WITH CORRESPONDING VIGNETTE NUMBERS

For

❧ Lynn, Jenny, and Jay ❧

Acknowledgments

The authors thank Dean Robert Reinstein of the Temple University Beasley School of Law for his support of this project.

Most importantly, we thank our Evidence students who inspired these materials and served as editors and "critiquers" of our work.

Anthony J. Bocchino
David A. Sonenshein
JoAnne A. Epps
Professors of Law, Temple University Beasley School of Law
2004

INTRODUCTION TO—

100 *Vignettes for Improving Trial Evidence Skills*

This book contains one hundred vignettes of trial testimony, designed to raise evidentiary issues in the context in which they occur. Each raises at least one evidentiary issue, although most vignettes have broader coverage.

Applications. These materials can be viewed in both an evidence or trial advocacy class, or as the basis for continuing legal education on evidence. In the law school setting, they will serve as supplementary materials, to be used in conjunction with a book, problem book, or casebook. The vignettes are examples of how specific evidentiary issues arise at trial, and provide a context for a better understanding of the rules of evidence as they are applied.

Case Synopsis. Each vignette begins with a short description of a lawsuit during which the vignette testimony occurs. A transcript of the text of a witness testimony in that lawsuit, in the question-and-answer format, follows.

Pauses. Periodic pauses are noted in each vignette. At each pause, consideration should be given as to whether an objection can be made to the questions, answers, or rulings that precede the response to that objection, and the proper ruling by a judge. If an objection would be properly sustained, consideration should then be given as to whether that objection could be cured by the laying of an evidentiary foundation.

Role Assignment. During class students will normally be assigned to play the roles of questioning attorney and witness. As the transcript is read, either a particular student or the rest of the class is assigned to make objections and arguments on those objections as necessary. If the objection is curable, questioning counsel is called upon to perform that function. The role of the judge is usually taken by the course instructor, but it can also be assigned.

Discussion. As the vignettes are played out in class, the student should stay in role as trial counsel make objections and arguments as they would in court. A full discussion raised by each vignette can occur at the end of the vignette or at each pause, at the option of the instruction. Space is provided on the materials for note-taking concerning objections, responses, and rulings.

Anthony J. Bocchino

Vignette
1

Judicial Notice—Fed. R. Evid. 201

The plaintiff, John Bernstein, has sued the defendant, Mary Wilson, for injuries he received when he was hit by her car as he crossed Main Street near the intersection of Seventh Avenue in Nita City. Bernstein claims that Wilson was negligent in that she was driving in excess of the 20 miles per hour speed limit that exists in all business districts in Nita City, and further that she was driving too fast for conditions. Wilson claims that Bernstein was responsible for his own injuries in that he crossed Main Street without using the crosswalk. The first witness for the plaintiff is Officer Nancy Wright who investigated the incident. We pick up in the midst of Officer Wright's testimony.

Q: Directing your attention to April 3, 2001, were you on duty that day?

A: Yes, I was working as a patrol officer on the 8 A.M. to 4 P.M. shift.

Q: What happened at approximately 3 P.M.?

A: I got a call to investigate a car-pedestrian accident near the intersection of Seventh and Main in Nita City.

Q: Have you ever been to that intersection before?

A: Yes, many times. It's in my patrol area.

Q: What is located at that intersection?

A: It is a mixed commercial and residential area.

Q: Your Honor, I ask that you take judicial notice of the fact that the intersection of Seventh Avenue and Main Street is a business district.

I *object, your Honor. May we offer evidence on this point?*

Judge: *Counselor, I've lived in Nita City all of my life and I can tell you from personal experience that the intersection of Seventh Avenue and Main Street is a business district.*

(Pause 1)

Q: What did you find at the intersection, Officer Wright?

A: The plaintiff, Mr. Bernstein, was lying on the pavement. He appeared to be unconscious. The defendant was standing near him.

Q: What were the weather conditions at that time?

A: I really don't remember.

Q: Your Honor, I ask that you take judicial notice of the fact that on April 3, 2001, it rained all afternoon in Nita City.

(Pause 2)

Q: Do you know the speed limit on Main Street at the intersection of Seventh Avenue?

A: I know what it is now but I can't be sure that it was the same three years ago.

Judge: *I drive by that intersection every day and the speed limit is 20 miles per hour. To save time, I'll take judicial notice of that fact.*

(Pause 3)

Vignette
2

Forms of Questions and Preserving Error—Fed. R. Evid. 103–104, 607, 611–612

On May 1 at approximately 11:30 A.M. the plaintiff, John Parsons, and the defendant, Rachel Dornan, were involved in a car accident at the intersection of 68th Street and Sherwood Avenue. The plaintiff claims that while the defendant was driving west on Sherwood Avenue in her Dodge van, she ran a red light and struck the plaintiff's Toyota, which was traveling north on 68th Street. The defendant claims that she entered the intersection on a yellow light and in fact the plaintiff ran the red light.

The first witness for the plaintiff is the plaintiff, John Parsons.

Q: What is your name?

A: John Parsons.

Q: Where do you live?

A: 7000 Greenhill Road here in town.

Q: And you've lived there for the past ten years?

(Pause 1)

A: That's right.

Q: What do you do for a living?

A: I work for the city as a maintenance worker. I've been doing that for eight years since I graduated from high school.

Q: Directing your attention to May 1st of last year at about 11:30 A.M., where were you?

A: In my car driving north on 68th Street in the city.

Q: How fast were you driving?

A: I can't put a number on it but not very fast.

(Pause 2)

Q: Were you driving within the posted speed limit of 35 miles per hour?

(Pause 3)

A: Sure, no question about it.

Q: Okay, what happened when you got to the intersection of 68th Street and Sherwood?

(Pause 4)

A: Well, as I approached the intersection the light was red for the northbound traffic, but about 100 feet before I reached Sherwood the light changed to green for the 68th Street traffic so I just kept on going.

Q: So you had the green light and weren't speeding?

(Pause 5)

A: Yes, definitely.

Q: What happened next?

A: Just as I entered the intersection that careless driver, Dornan, in the Dodge van hit my car as she drove from east to west into the intersection.

(Pause 6)

Q: What part of your car did the defendant hit when she ran the red light?

A: The right front quarter panel.

Q: Did you get the car repaired?

A: Yes, of course.

Q: How much did it cost to repair the car?

A: I don't remember specifically.

Q: Would it refresh your recollection if I told you it was $1,420.50?

(Pause 7)

A: No, but it's on the bill from the repair shop.

Q: Showing you that bill do you now remember the specific amount?

(Pause 8)

A: (Reading from bill) Yes, it says here $1,420.50.

(Pause 9)

Cross-examination of the plaintiff, Parsons.

Q: You aren't sure about your exact speed at the time of the accident, are you?

A: Well I know that I was going under the speed limit.

(Pause 10)

Q: You were on your way to a doctor's appointment at the time of the accident?

A: That's right.

Q: The appointment was for 11:30, wasn't it?

A: Yes, but he's always late.

(Pause 11)

Q: You were going to see the doctor for migraine headaches, right?

A: Yes.

Q: A dog crossed your path right before the accident, correct?

A: Yes.

Q: You swerved to avoid the dog, right?

A: Yes, but that didn't have anything to do with the accident.

(Pause 12)

Q: But in addition to being late for a doctor's appointment and suffering a migraine headache, you did swerve to avoid the dog, didn't you?

(Pause 13)

Vignette
3

Form of Questions and Preserving Error—Fed. R. Evid. 103–104, 607, 611–612

The plaintiff, Maria Rodriguez, has sued the defendant, Business Machines Incorporated (BMI), for discrimination on the basis of gender and national origin in the making of a promotion decision. She claims that she was passed over for a promotion to Assistant Vice-President for Sales from her position as Sales Manager for the Eastern Region of BMI because of her national origin. The events underlying this cause of action happened in 2002. The plaintiff is the first witness at trial.

Q: Please state your name and address for the record.

A: Maria Rodriguez, 7000 Sherwood Lane, Nita City, Nita.

Q: What is your occupation?

A: I am the Sales Manager for the Eastern Region of BMI.

Q: You've had that position for six years, haven't you?

(Pause 1)

A: Yes.

Q: What education do you have that prepared you for that position?

A: I graduated from the Nita City public schools, and received my BS in business and MBA from Nita University.

Q: I take it from your last response that you are a lifelong resident of Nita City?

Objection, leading.

(Pause 2)

A: Yes, that's right.

Q: When did you start working for BMI?

A: In 1989, after I received my MBA.

Q: How many promotions have you received at BMI?

(Pause 3)

A: Four; from Sales Assistant, to Assistant Sales Manager, to Division Sales Manager, to Assistant Regional Sales Manager, to Regional Sales Manager—my current position.

(By defendant's counsel): Objection, I move to strike everything after the word "four" as non-responsive.

(Pause 4)

Q: Is Assistant Vice-President for Sales the next position up the chain of responsibility from your current position?

(Pause 5)

A: Yes.

Q: Directing your attention to August 2002, did you apply for the position of Assistant Vice-President of Sales at BMI?

A: Yes.

Q: Did you fill out the necessary papers and forward them to the powers that be?

(Pause 6)

A: Yes, I followed the procedure set out in the position announcement.

Q: What papers did you have to submit to the President of BMI?

(Pause 7)

A: A resume and a brief statement of what I felt were my qualifications for the position.

Q: Was the next step in the process to go through interviews?

(Pause 8)

A: Yes.

Q: What happened during the interviewing process?

(Pause 9)

A: The first round of interviews were routine. The questions were tough, but fair, and I was confident that I was doing pretty well. The next and final step was an interview with the President, Mr. Stenton. During that interview he seemed to be very interested in my personal background, my family, where I grew up, my language facility. I'm fluent in Spanish as well as English. I didn't think much of it at the time, but when a white male got the job who had been a Regional Sales Manager for three years fewer than I had, I thought back on the interview with Stenton and got quite angry. I later heard through the grapevine that Stenton and the new Assistant Vice-President were members of the same club that doesn't admit anyone whose parents didn't come over on the Mayflower, and I put two and two together.

(Pause 10)

Q: In any of your previous promotions was your ethnicity considered in the way it was in this interview?

(Pause 11)

A: Not to my knowledge. I'd received every promotion I applied for up until this one.

Q: So it wasn't, then?

(Pause 12)

A: Right.

Q: So your ethnicity was never considered in previous promotion considerations, then?

(Pause 13)

A: That's right. Those decisions were on the merits.

The direct examination of plaintiff Rodriguez continued and was completed. We now pick up as her cross-examination begins.

Q: You have worked for BMI for fifteen years, haven't you?

A: Yes.

Q: During those fifteen years you have received four promotions?

A: Yes.

Q: You are thirty-nine years old, aren't you?

A: Yes.

Q: *That makes you the youngest Regional Sales Manager at BMI, isn't that right?*

Objection, that assumes a fact not in evidence.

(Pause 14)

Q: The man who received the promotion to Assistant Vice-President for Sales when you applied for that job was forty-five years old at the time, wasn't he?

A: Yes, but I had more experience at BMI.

(Pause 15)

Q: He was hired to work at BMI after a twenty-year career at RCA, wasn't he?

A: That's right.

Q: His last position at RCA, which he held for eight years before joining BMI, was the equivalent of your position, wasn't it?

(Pause 16)

A: Roughly equivalent but not exactly so. My region is larger than his was at RCA.

(By defendant's counsel) Move to strike the last answer as non-responsive. The question could easily be answered yes or no.

(Pause 17)

Q: So the person who got the job was older than you and had more experience than you, isn't that right?

(Pause 18)

A: And he was a white male from the right club.

(Pause 19)

Q: When you applied for this promotion, Ms. Rodriguez, you submitted a statement of why you were qualified for the Assistant Vice-President for Sales position, didn't you?

A: Yes.

Q: You mentioned how you worked your way through college and graduate school?

A: Yes.

Q: You wrote of growing up in a largely poor, Spanish-speaking neighborhood?

A: Yes, to show my ability to work hard for my goals.

Q: You also wrote of your being bilingual?

A: Yes, I believe that's an asset.

Q: All of these factors were mentioned by you, weren't they?

A: Yes.

Q: But when Mr. Stenton asked your about your personal and family background and the fact of your being bilingual he was discriminating against you, right?

(Pause 20)

A: It was the way he asked in a condescending way.

Q: Just a few more questions, Ms. Rodriguez. You have received four promotions at BMI, haven't you?

A: Yes

Q: You've only applied for five promotions, correct?

A: Yes.

Q: Isn't it possible, Ms. Rodriguez, that this one time when you didn't get the promotion you just weren't qualified, but you brought this lawsuit to mask that fact?

(Pause 21)

Vignette
4

Form of Questions and Preserving Error—Fed. R. Evid. 103–104, 607, 611–612

Plaintiff sues Defendant, alleging that Plaintiff, a pedestrian, was injured on July 1, 2003 when Defendant ran a red light and hit her with his automobile at the intersection of Fourth and Main streets in the city. Defendant claims that Plaintiff ran out into the intersection in violation of a red light and a "Don't Walk" signal. Plaintiff calls an eyewitness, Jane Wylie, to testify to her observations of the collision.

Direct Examination

Q: What is your name?

A: Jane Wylie.

Q: Where do you live?

A: I live at 435 Main Street in this city.

Q: And you have lived there for seventeen years haven't you?

Objection.

(Pause 1)

A: Yes.

Q: Directing your attention to July 1, 2003, you were at home at the corner of Fourth and Main streets that day, weren't you?

Objection.

(Pause 2)

A: Yes, I was.

Q: Tell me what you saw that day.

Objection.

(Pause 3)

A: I saw that reckless Defendant run a red light, going about 50 miles per hour.

Move to Strike.

(Pause 4)

Q: Now, after colliding with the plaintiff, what did the defendant do?

Objection.

(Pause 5)

A: He slowed down for a second or two and then sped away.

Q: Ms. Wylie, what was the license tag number of the car which ran the red light?

A: I can't remember.

Q: (Approaching the witness) Showing you Plaintiff's Exhibit 1 for identification, does it refresh your recollection as to license number?

A: It does. (Reading from Exhibit 1) It was SAP 156.

Move to Strike.

(Pause 6)

Cross-Examination

Q: Ms. Wylie, you wear glasses don't you?

Objection, leading.

(Pause 7)

A: Yes.

Q: You have 20/100 vision in both eyes don't you?

A: Yes.

Q: But you weren't wearing your glasses on July 1, 2003 were you?

A: No, but I was close enough to the intersection to see it clearly without my glasses.

Move to Strike.

(Pause 8)

Q: But you weren't wearing your glasses were you?

Objection, Asked and Answered.

(Pause 9)

A: No.

Q: At the time of the accident, you were babysitting, weren't you?

A: Yes, I was.

Q: You were babysitting for your four-year-old nephew, weren't you?

A: Yes.

Q: And he was playing on the sidewalk, wasn't he?

A: Yes.

Q: And you were watching him and reading the newspaper?

Objection.

(Pause 10)

A: Yes.

Q: So, given that you were watching your nephew, reading the paper, and not wearing your glasses at the time of the accident, there was no way you could have seen the accident, is there?

Objection.

(Pause 11)

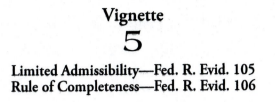

Vignette

5

Limited Admissibility—Fed. R. Evid. 105
Rule of Completeness—Fed. R. Evid. 106

The plaintiff, Charlotte Hennessey, claims she was injured when she slipped and fell in the parking lot of the defendant, Nita Building Supplies Store, in Nita City. The fall occurred in a portion of the lot adjacent to where a repair crew from the Nita Excavation Company, another defendant, was replacing some curbing. Nita Building Supplies claims that the plaintiff failed to look where she was going, and in the alternative, that it had no notice of the depression in the parking lot, and further, that the depression in their parking lot where Plaintiff fell was caused by the carelessness of the crew of the Nita Excavation Company. The first witness for the plaintiff is her husband, who was with the plaintiff when she was injured. We pick up in the midst of the direct examination of Harold Hennessey.

Q: What happened after your wife fell?

A: I got there as she was lying on the ground so I didn't actually see her fall. It was obvious that her ankle was either broken or badly sprained. I called for an ambulance and my wife was taken to the hospital. My daughter, who was with us, went to the hospital with her.

Q: What did you do?

A: I went over to a Nita Excavation construction worker who was replacing some curbing near where Charlotte fell and asked him what had happened.

Q: What did he say to you?

A: He said that he saw what had happened and that he was sorry, but the pavement where she fell had been damaged by a Nita Excavation back hoe three days earlier. He said that he had put a cone over the depression but that he had seen it being removed by the Nita Building Supplies Store manager the day before.

Counsel for Nita Building Supplies: Move to strike the answer.

(Pause 1)

Mr. Hennessey completed his direct examination. We pick up in the midst of his cross-examination by counsel for Nita Building Supplies.

Q: You said on direct examination that it was obvious that your wife's ankle was broken or severely sprained, didn't you?

A: Yes, it was.

Q: Didn't you give a written statement to the manager of the Nita Building Supplies store on the day of this incident?

A: Yes, I did.

Q: Showing you Exhibit 17, that's your statement, isn't it?

A: Yes it is.

Q: Doesn't your statement say about your wife's claimed injury, "I'm not sure how badly she's hurt, but she has been taken to the hospital.'

Plaintiff's counsel: Objection. Motion to Strike as hearsay.

Q: Your Honor, this is not offered for the truth of the matter asserted.

Judge: Objection overruled.

(Pause 2)

Plaintiff's counsel: May we approach the bench your Honor.

(Pause 3)

Vignette
6

Competency—Fed. R. Evid. 601–602

Patricia Jones was killed and her son, Jason, suffered a brain injury, when the engine of a small boat in which she and her son were riding exploded. Her estate brought suit against the manufacturer of the boat and the designer of the engine. The defendants have denied liability, claiming that the engine exploded when hit by lightning. The plaintiff's first-witness is Jason, son of the decedent. Jason is now six years old; he was four at the time of the explosion. We join the trial at the beginning of Jason's direct examination.

Q: Tell us your name.

A: Jason Jones.

Q: Where do you live?

A: Center City.

Q: Do you live on Eighth Street?

(Pause 1)

A: I don't know. I live in Center City.

Q: Jason, how old are you now?

A: Six.

Q: Can you count it on your fingers?

A: One, two, three, four, five, six.

Q: Jason, do you know where you are?

A: Yes.

Q: Where?

A: Court.

Q: Jason, do you know that if you don't tell the truth here today, bad things will happen to you?

(Pause 2)

A: Yes.

Q: What is the difference between telling the truth and telling a lie?

A: Telling the truth is good; lying is not good.

Q: What does it mean to tell a lie?

A: It's when I don't tell my daddy something.

Q: Jason, I know this is hard, but I want you to think back to the day your mom died. Do you remember that day?

Defense Attorney: Make I take the witness on voir dire?

Judge: Yes, you may.

Q: Jason, after the explosion, you woke up in the hospital, didn't you?

A: Yes.

Q: And you found out you had been asleep for several days, didn't you?

A: Yes.

Q: And at first you didn't remember what happened in the boat, did you?

A: No.

Q: And it was only after you talked to your dad that you knew what happened to your mom, wasn't it?

A: I guess so.

(At the bench) Defense Attorney: Your Honor, we object. This witness is not competent to testify.

(Pause 3)

Questioning continues by the prosecutor:

Q: What's the difference between telling the truth and telling a lie?

A: The truth is real; a lie is when you make something up.

Q: What happens if you tell a lie?

A: My dad makes me go to my room.

Prosecutor: Your Honor, will the court now allow the witness to testify about the events at issue?

Defense Attorney: Your Honor, we renew our objection. This witness has still not been shown to be competent to testify.

(Pause 4)

Vignette
7

Lay Opinions—Fed. R. Evid. 701

On July 14, 2003, Jack Meade was killed in an auto accident while a passenger in Fred Haskell's car. The accident occurred on a rainy and foggy night. The car evidently skidded off the road and ran into a tree, killing both driver Haskell and his passenger, Meade. Meade's estate brings a wrongful-death action against Haskell's estate.

The plaintiff calls Rhonda Carter, a part-time auto mechanic, who was nearby at the time of the crash.

Q: Please state your name and address.

A: My name is Rhonda Carter and I live at Highway 47 in Centerville.

Q: How old are you?

A: Twenty.

Q: What do you do for a living?

A: I'm an auto mechanic.

Q: Directing your attention to 11 P.M. on the evening of July 14, 2003, where were you?

A: I was in bed reading.

Q: Where in the house is your bedroom located?

A: In the front left of the second floor, about 30 feet from the road.

Q: While reading at 11 P.M. on the night of July 14, did you hear anything?

A: I heard a crash right in front of my house.

Q: After hearing the crash, what did you do?

A: I looked out the window and saw that a car had hit a big elm tree right in front of my house.

Q: Did you hear anything directly before the collision occurred?

A: Yes.

Q: What did you hear?

A: Well, I was sitting in bed reading and I heard this car on the highway. I heard the engine gunning—you know, really racing.

(Pause 1)

Q: Did you hear anything else?

A: Yes, I heard the tires squealing as if the car was out of control.

(Pause 2)

Q: Then what happened?

A: I heard the car smash against the tree with a loud crash.

Q: Based on everything you heard, how fast was the car going?

(Pause 3)

Vignette
8

Lay Opinion Testimony—Fed. R. Evid. 701

Plaintiff George Atkins sues Defendant Lucy Davis for personal injuries arising from an automobile collision. At trial, Plaintiff calls James Carter, a passenger in the defendant's car, as a witness. We pick up in the midst of Carter's testimony.

Q: Mr. Carter, do you know the defendant, Lucy Davis?

A: Yes, we have worked in the same office for two years.

Q: Did you see her on the day of the accident?

A: Yes, we left work together at 5:30 and stopped for drinks at a tavern near the office.

Q: How many drinks did she have?

Objection. Assumes facts not in evidence.

(Pause 1)

A: Two whiskey sours.

Q: When did you leave the bar?

A: At approximately 6 P.M.

Q: What did you do?

A: We got into her car and began to drive home. She was going to drop me off at my house.

Q: What happened next?

A: Just after we pulled away from the curb, we crashed into the plaintiff's car.

Q: Do you have an opinion as to the state of the defendant's sobriety when you left the bar?

A: Yes, she was drunk.

Move to strike the answer as an improper lay opinion.

(Pause 2)

Q: At the time when the crash occurred, was the defendant driving at an excessive rate of speed?

Objection, improper opinion.

(Pause 3)

A: Yes.

Q: Did you see the plaintiff after the collision?

A: Yes, I jumped out of the car and ran to his car to see if he was injured.

Q: When you got to his car, what did you see?

A: He looked very frightened and was in a lot of pain.

Objection, move to strike the answer as an improper opinion.

(Pause 4)

Vignette
9

Lay Opinion Testimony—Fed. R. Evid. 701

Mary Parkinson has sued her employer, the Nita Fire and Casualty Insurance Company, for gender discrimination. She claims that she was not taken seriously in her job, was sexually harassed, evaluated unfairly, and passed over for promotion because of her gender. She further claims that a promotion for which she was qualified was given to a less-experienced and less-qualified male employee of the company. Parkinson calls as a witness one of her supervisors, Wendy Williams. Relevant portions of Ms. Williams's testimony on direct examination follow.

Q: Please introduce yourself to the jury.

A: My name is Wendy Williams and I live here in Nita City at 25 Woodbine Avenue.

Q: Are you employed?

A: Yes, I work as a claims analyst supervisor for the Nita Fire and Casualty Company.

Q: Do you know Mary Parkinson?

A: Yes, she works at NF&C in the same department as me. I am one of her supervisors.

Q: Does she report directly to you?

A: No. She reports to Fred Forrest. He is responsible for her direct supervision.

Q: Is he also responsible for evaluating her job performance and making recommendations for promotions?

A: Yes. It is his primary responsibility although all evaluations and promotions for the department are recommended by a three person committee consisting of Fred, David Dornan, and me.

Q: So have you reviewed Ms. Parkinson's work over the years?

A: Yes, she's an excellent worker and a top performer.

(Pause 1)

Q: Have you seen Mr. Forrest interacting with Ms. Parkinson?

A: You can't miss it, our area is an open one with the people at Ms. Parkinson's level in open desks and the offices of Forrest, Dornan, and myself on the side of the room in semi-private cubicles.

Q: What does that mean?

A: The cubicles have doors on them, although they're usually kept open and the walls don't go to the ceiling. If you listen carefully you can hear what's going on in the adjoining cubicles. I am in between Forrest and Dornan and often can overhear conversations in their cubicles, especially if voices are raised.

Q: Where is Ms. Parkinson's work station in relation to your office?

A: Fifteen feet away, directly in my sight.

(Pause 2)

Q: What have you seen or heard regarding the interaction between Forrest and Ms. Parkinson?

A: He's always leaning on her desk talking to her, or sitting on her desk so he's above her. It often looks like he's trying to look down her blouse.

(Pause 3)

Q: What have you seen about his facial expression?

A: He gets this smirk on his face and he kind of leers.

(Pause 4)

Q: Has Forrest ever placed his hands on Ms. Parkinson?

A: Many times. I've seen him with his hands on her shoulders standing behind her as she's seated, touching her arm, her waist. Once I even saw him place his hand on her buttocks.

Q: How has Ms. Parkinson reacted to Forrest touching her?

A: She's upset and obviously uncomfortable.

(Pause 5)

Q: How so?

A: She'll twist away from him, or push his hand off of her, or if she's sitting, she'll stand up. I've seen her rush out of the room. Once I followed her to the women's room and saw her crying.

(Pause 6)

Q: Have you overheard any conversation between Forrest and Ms. Parkinson?

A: Several times. I've heard Forrest ask Ms. Parkinson out on dates, even asked her once to spend a weekend with him at his lake cottage.

Q: How did Ms. Parkinson react to these suggestions?

A: She made it clear she wasn't interested. Forrest is married; he should be ashamed of himself. Of course Ms. Parkinson rejected him.

(Pause 7)

Q: Any other conversation you've overheard?

A: The most recent was during the evaluation period six months ago. Forrest met with Ms. Parkinson in his office. I could overhear the whole thing. Forrest said he was going to evaluate Ms. Parkinson's work as 'Satisfactory' on our 'Excellent,' 'Good,' 'Satisfactory,' and 'Unacceptable' scale. In our system that's a low evaluation. Ms. Parkinson was upset and she asked him why so low an evaluation of her work. Forrest then said that if she were more collegial that her evaluation could be adjusted up, and depending on how collegial she became her evaluation could reach the "excellent" level. Ms. Parkinson asked how she could do that and Forrest said she could start by joining him for dinner that night. Ms. Parkinson got real angry and left the office. I could see she was upset. Who wouldn't be?

(Pause 8)

Q: Did you independently review and evaluate Ms. Parkinson's work product?

A: I did and it compared favorably to that of other people in the office, including James Wilson, who received an "Excellent" rating from Forrest and was recently promoted.

Q: Why wasn't Ms. Parkinson promoted instead of Mr. Wilson?

A: Because of Forrest's evaluation. She rejected him and he discriminated against her. It's an old story unfortunately often told.

(Pause 9)

Q: Does Forrest still supervise Ms. Parkinson?

A: No, after she complained to our human relations department, I became Ms. Parkinson's supervisor and Forrest is not allowed to interact with her or participate in her evaluations.

(Pause 10)

Vignette
10
Lay Opinions—Fed. R. Evid. 701

Jerry Shields, a municipal employee, was killed while operating an aerial lift manufactured by Artos Corporation, that he used in a tree-trimming operation. Shields' Estate filed a wrongful-death action against Artos for defective manufacture of the lift, and Artos filed a third-party action for indemnity against Bascom, the manufacturer of the boom cylinder containing the piston rod that allegedly fractured and caused the accident. At the trial, the Shields' Estate called Ralph Rogers as a witness.

Q: Please state your name and address, sir.

A: I am Ralph Rogers. I live at 234 River Road in the city.

Q: Mr. Rogers, what do you do for a living?

A: I have been a fleet maintenance supervisor for this municipality for the past fifteen years. I had held that position for eleven years at the time of the accident.

Q: Did you know the decedent, Jerry Shields?

A: Yes, he had worked for me for at least seven years.

Q: Did you see him on the day of the accident?

A: Yes, I was called to the scene right after it occurred.

Q: When you arrived on the scene, what did you see?

A: Jerry was in tremendous pain.

Move to strike.

(Pause 1)

Q: What else did you notice?

A: He was scared and agitated.

Move to strike.

(Pause 2)

Q: Now you mentioned that you are a fleet supervisor. Describe your duties.

A: I was and am responsible for all city equipment, including the aerial life involved in this case, and I am in charge of purchasing, maintenance and repair of all the equipment.

Q: Are you familiar with the aerial lift which fractured here?

A: Yes, I purchased it. In addition, after the accident my employees and I took it apart and inspected its boom assembly. It appeared to me that the lower boom assembly had fractured at a point where a hole is drilled in the threaded end of a rod and a pin inserted through the hole. In my opinion, the fracture was caused by metal fatigue and was attributable to the design of the rod. The accident was caused by two things. First, the hole in the pin caused the rod to be weakened and second, the threads on the rod itself caused the breaking point. They were sharp and it broke right at the point where all those things intersected. I have never seen a cylinder configured that way.

Move to strike.

(Pause 3)

Vignette
11

Expert Opinions—Fed. R. Evid. 702

Madeline Hart was kidnapped three years ago by a group of terrorists. She is now on trial for the part she played in an armed robbery during the time she was kidnapped. Her defense is that she was coerced to commit the crime by her kidnappers.

In its case in chief, the prosecution produced a writing that stated that Hart wished to overthrow capitalist society and that she would rob a bank to accomplish this goal. The prosecution called a handwriting expert who testified that the incriminating statement was undoubtedly written by Hart. To diminish the effect of the incriminating statement, the defense calls Dr. Margaret Singer who claims to be an expert in the field of psycholinguistics.

Defense Counsel: *Your Honor, at this time, the defense calls Dr. Margaret Singer, whom we will qualify as an expert in the field of psycholinguistics.*

Judge: *Counsel, call Dr. Singer.*

Defense Counsel: *Thank you, your Honor.*

Q: Please state your name and profession.

A: I am Dr. Margaret Singer and I am a practicing psychologist.

Q: What is your educational background?

A: I received bachelors degrees in psychology and linguistics from Stanford University. I received a masters and a Ph.D. in psychology from the University of Michigan, where I was Magna Cum Laude.

Q: Are you a member of any professional societies?

A: Yes. I am a member of the American Psychological Association. I am a member of the league of Therapeutic Psychologists, and right now I am President of the National Society for the Study of Psycholinguistics.

Q: When did you become president of the Society?

A: Two years ago, in 2002. I am one of the founding members.

Q: What is "Psycholinguistics"?

A: Psycholinguistics is the study of how the human mind selects words for the purpose of expression. I and three other prominent psychologists formulated this theory around twelve years ago after extensive experimentation proved that every person has an idiosyncratic method of choosing words. By use of the accepted testing procedures in psycholinguistics, we can compare the normal word choice patterns of a client to another exemplar to determine if the exemplar was actually produced by the client in a voluntary way.

Q: To what extent is psycholinguistics a recognized field of expertise?

A: I have been to many conferences. It is the subject of discussion in many professional circles, among both psychologists and linguists. And among psychologists, psycholinguistics is thought to be a well-regarded subspecialty.

Q: Is psycholinguistic analysis capable of replication or verification?

A: Yes.

Q: Dr. Singer, please tell us your opinion of whether the writing attributed to the defendant was written voluntarily.

(Pause 1)

Vignette
12

Expert Opinions—Fed. R. Evid. 702

Esther Worthy was mugged two years ago and later identified a suspect in a one-on-one show-up at a police station. Based on the station house identification and certain other circumstantial evidence, the government charged William James with the crimes arising from the mugging, armed robbery and assault with a dangerous weapon.

The victim, Ms. Worthy, described the crime as having taken place at approximately 2 A.M. in a fairly secluded area that was not well lighted. Ms. Worthy had never seen Mr. James before, and the entire incident, including the robbery at gunpoint and the assault that followed, took no more than 3–4 minutes.

Defense Counsel: *Your Honor, I would like to call Dr. Ezra Lopatin, whom we will qualify as a psychologist and expert in the field of eyewitness identification and the problems associated with it.*

Judge: *Counsel, call Dr. Lopatin.*

Defense Counsel: *Thank you, your Honor.*

Q: Please state your name.

A: Dr. Ezra Lopatin.

Q: What do you do for a living?

A: I am a clinical and research psychologist.

Q: What is your educational background?

A: I received a bachelor of science degree in Psychology from Wesleyan University and a Ph.D. In Psychology from Cornell University.

Q: Are you a member of any professional organizations?

A: Yes, I am a member of the American Psychological Association and I am the founder and President of the Society for the Study of Eyewitness Identification.

Q: Have you developed a specialty in the study of eyewitness identification?

A: I have.

Q: Tell the court about the study of eyewitness identification.

A: Over the last ten years or so, a number of psychologists have studied the accuracy of, and the factors which affect the accuracy of, eyewitness identification. Over the years, some psychologists, like me, have studied the impact of suggestiveness, level of detail, impact of the presence of a weapon, and other factors which bear on the reliability of eyewitness identifications. Much of what we have learned is counter-intuitive. For example, the lack of any relationship between the level of certainty of the identification and its accuracy.

Q: To what extent is the study of expert identification a recognized field of expertise?

A: I have been to many conferences. It is the subject of discussion in many professional circles, among both psychologists and criminologists. And among psychologists, it is an increasingly recognized sub-speciality.

Q: Is the study of expert identification analysis capable of replication or verification?

A: Not with the precision of science, no. Preliminary studies, however, have found a significant correlation between the results of expert identification analysis and criminal trial outcomes.

Q: Your Honor, I offer Dr. Lopatin as an expert psychologist, qualified to render an opinion on the factors that the jury should consider in evaluating the eyewitness identification in this case, and an opinion on the reliability of the victim's identification.

Objection.

(Pause 1)

Vignette
13

Opinions: Lay and Expert—Fed. R. Evid. 702–705

The children of Marvin Dixon have brought a cause of action to set aside the December 25, 2000 will of their deceased father that leaves the entirety of his estate to the Nita Humane Society. They seek to set aside the will on the ground that Mr. Dixon lacked the testamentary capacity to execute the will. The children call as a witness Dr. Joyce Martinez, a psychiatrist. We pick up in the midst of Dr. Martinez' testimony after she has completed stating her qualifications.

Q: *Your Honor, I offer Dr. Martinez as an expert witness in the field of medicine with a specialization in psychiatry and ask that she be qualified to render an opinion as to the testamentary capacity of Mr. Marvin Dixon at the time that he executed the will in question in this case.*

(Pause 1)

Judge: *Hearing no objection, she may be so qualified.*

Q: *Your Honor, will you take judicial notice that the legal definition for testamentary capacity is whether the testator had the mental ability to know what he was doing when he wrote the will, knew the effect of his acts in making the will, realized what he was doing, knew his relatives and knew the property he owned?*

(Pause 2)

Judge: *That is the legal definition in Nita and I do take judicial notice of that definition.*

Q: Dr. Martinez, are you aware of the legal definition of testamentary capacity as judicially noticed by the judge?

A: Yes.

Q: Dr. Martinez, have you come to an opinion as to whether Marvin Dixon possessed the testamentary capacity to execute a will as of December 25, 2000?

(Pause 3)

A: Yes I have. In my opinion, Mr. Marvin Dixon did not possess the testamentary capacity to execute a will as of December 25, 2000.

Q: On what do you base that opinion?

A: I have reviewed Mr. Dixon's medical records from the Nita Gerontology Center where he was living from January 1998 until his death on March 15, 2003 and I have talked to a number of family members who were in contact with him during that period of time.

Q: Is this the type of information that you normally rely on in coming to an opinion such as the one you have given today?

(Pause 4)

A: It is not unusual in situations where I was not the treating physician to use such information, yes. Usually, the treating psychiatrist has better information because of personal interaction with the patient but in cases like this where the treating psychiatrist, Dr. Gordon, is deceased, I can use the information I referred to in coming to an opinion as to the mental state of a patient who I have not met personally.

(Pause 5)

Q: What do the medical records for Mr. Dixon show regarding his condition on December 24 and 25, 2000?

A: A night nurse reports that Mr. Dixon became distressed on the evening of December 24, 2000 after watching an animated cartoon presentation of the poem *The Night Before Christmas*. The nurse states that Mr. Dixon seemed—and I'm using the nurse's words—'sad and depressed.' The nurse also notes that Mr. Dixon had difficulty walking from the TV room to his bedroom and had to be helped into his bed.

(Pause 6)

Q: Is there anything else in the records for those dates?

A: Yes, Dr. Gordon notes in the record for December 25, 2000 that Mr. Dixon became agitated and demanded to see his lawyer on Christmas morning. Apparently the lawyer came to see Mr. Dixon because Dr. Gordon reports that after being visited by a Ms. Carter, who I now know was Mr. Dixon's lawyer, that he calmed down. Dr. Gordon wrote in the record that in her opinion Mr. Dixon, who was a manic depressive, apparently moved from a depressive state in the morning to a manic state in the afternoon.

(Pause 7)

Q: What did you learn from Mr. Dixon's children?

A: Mary Dixon visited her father on Christmas morning and she told me that her father was quite anxious and appeared angry. She said that her father asked, 'who takes care of them the rest of the year,' with no apparent reference to anyone or anything.

(Pause 8)

Q: Did any other of Mr. Dixon's children provide you with any information?

A: Yes, Marvin, Jr. visited his father on Christmas afternoon. During the visit his father was cheerful—in his son's words, 'almost elated.' Mr. Dixon, Sr. told his son and his grandson who was also present, not to worry about the reindeer, that he had taken care of them. Marvin Jr. didn't know what his father meant, but he did say that his son, Marvin III, seemed quite happy at the news.

(Pause 9)

Q: What does all this mean, Dr. Martinez?

A: In my opinion, Mr. Davis became worried about the wellbeing of Santa's reindeer after watching the television animation of the poem, *The Night Before Christmas*, called his lawyer the next day, and changed his will to leave his estate to the Nita Humane Society to provide for their care.

(Pause 10)

Vignette
14

Expert Opinions (Basis)—Fed. R. Evid. 703, 803(18)

Plaintiff George Watson has sued Defendant Leslie Forrest for personal injuries arising from an automobile accident. Watson has also joined as a defendant an emergency room physician, Dr. Rhonda Wilson, claiming malpractice in the post-accident medical treatment he received from Dr. Wilson.

At trial, Plaintiff offered evidence that he was perfectly healthy at the time of the accident, and had no pre-existing conditions that had any relevance to the lawsuit.

The defendants call Dr. August Johnson as an expert witness. We pick up in the midst of Dr. Johnson's testimony.

Q: Now, Dr. Johnson, in reaching your opinion as to the cause of Mr. Watson's injuries and the propriety of the treatment he received, what did you do?

A: First, I spoke on the telephone to his family physician, Dr. Ruth Morris.

Q: Why did you do that?

A: Because getting a medical history is indispensable to making a diagnosis.

Q: What did the family physician, Dr. Morris tell you?

Objection, hearsay.

(Pause 1)

Q: Did you do anything else?

A: Yes, I reviewed the patient's fifteen-year-old X-rays and the accompanying letter from the radiologist.

Q: Did you speak with the radiologist?

A: No, he died about ten years ago and his practice was closed.

Q: What did the X-rays and report reveal?

Objection. Hearsay.

(Pause 2)

Q: Did you speak to anyone else in order to reach your opinion in this case?

A: Well, of course, I spoke to the patient, himself.

Q: What did the patient, the plaintiff, tell you?

Objection. Hearsay.

(Pause 3)

Q: Did you consult any books or treatises before formulating your opinion?

A: Yes, I consulted the treatise, entitled "Injuries to the Neck and Back" by Franklin and Schwartz.

Q: Is the Franklin and Schwartz treatise authoritative in the field of diagnosis and treatment for back injuries?

A: It is.

Q: Your Honor, I offer the Franklin and Schwartz treatise into evidence.

Objection. The book is hearsay and cannot be admitted in evidence.

(Pause 4)

Vignette
15

Expert Opinions (Basis)—Fed. R. Evid. 703–704

Plaintiff Jack Peters sues the defendant municipality for alleged misconduct committed by the municipality's police officers. Plaintiff claims that the police officers used excessive force in effecting an arrest of the plaintiff, and that the arrest was not based on probable cause. The municipality cannot be held liable unless the fact-finder determines that the municipality, through its training or supervision, manifested a willful disregard for the civil rights of its citizens. Plaintiff calls Marie Wilson, a former police captain who now serves as an expert in police misconduct cases. We pick up in the midst of Ms. Wilson's testimony, after she was found to have been qualified as an expert.

Q: Ms. Wilson, do you have an opinion as to quality of the supervision in this municipality's police department during the period when the events in this case took place?

A: I do.

Q: Before telling us that opinion, tell the jury how you arrived at it.

A: I studied the report of the police consultant who happened to have studied the department at about the time of the incident in this case. The report stated that discipline and supervision had basically broken down in the department.

Move to strike the last sentence as hearsay and lacking in personal knowledge.

(Pause 1)

Q: Now, what is your opinion on the quality of discipline in the department?

A: Discipline was lax and ineffectual.

Q: Based on your experience, training, and study of the municipality's police department, do you have an opinion as to whether the municipality's operation of its police department demonstrated a willful disregard for the rights of its citizens?

A: I do.

Q: What is that opinion?

Objection.

(Pause 2)

Vignette
16

Expert Opinion (basis)—Fed. R. Evid. 703

The plaintiff, Acme Paper Company, has sued the Barton Fire and Casualty Company, the defendant, for payment pursuant to a fire insurance policy written by the defendant on the plaintiff's factory on 111 Main Street which was totally destroyed by fire on February 10, 2004. Barton defends, alleging that the fire was a result of arson by Jay Carlton, an employee of Acme, who set the fire at the behest of the owners of the Acme Paper Company.

The parties stipulated that the fire occurred and that the Acme factory was completely destroyed. The burden of proving arson is on the defendant. The defendant calls as its first witness Frank Grant, a Fire Marshal who investigated the fire. The parties have stipulated that Grant is an expert witness in the field of fire investigation and is qualified to give an opinion as to the cause of the fire.

The direct examination of Grant continues.

Q: Were you on duty on February 10, 2004 at about 10 P.M.?

A: Yes, I was called to investigate a fire at the Acme Paper Company at 111 Main Street.

Q: What did you do?

A: I talked to the firefighters who were at the scene, specifically to Donna Potter, who was the firefighter in charge.

Q: Why did you talk to her?

A: To get information necessary for my investigation.

Q: What did she tell you?

A: She said that the fire had spread very rapidly from the time she arrived on the scene at 9 P.M.

(Pause 1)

Q.   Did she tell you anything else?

A: Yes, she said that she took the call reporting the fire at 8:42 P.M. from a witness named George Jackson. Jackson told her that he saw flames coming out of the windows on the first, third, and fifth floors of the building as he drove by at about 8:30 P.M.

(Pause 2)

Q: What was the significance of Jackson's report?

A: His report showed that there were three separate and non-communicating fires at the same time, which is a strong indicator of arson. The recognized authority on fire investigations, Jane Byrne, says in her book *Fire Investigation* that where there are separate and non-communicating fires in a building, arson is indicated.

(Pause 3)

Q: Is Ms. Byrne's book recognized by fire investigators as an authoritative text?

A: Yes, it's the bible for us.

Q: Your Honor, I ask that Byrne's book *Fire Investigation*, which has been marked as Defendant's Exhibit 1 for identification, be accepted in evidence and I request permission to publish Chapter 4, Section 12 of that book, which deals with separate and non-communicating fires, to the jury.

(Pause 4)

The direct examination of Grant continued and he gave the opinion that the Acme fire was the result of arson. We pick up in the midst of the cross-examination of Grant.

Q: You inspected the Acme building after the fire was put out, didn't you? .

A: Yes.

Q: You found out that the electrical wiring for the first, third and fifth floors was all on the same circuit, isn't that right?

A: Yes.

Q: You discovered that there was faulty wiring in the circuit, didn't you?

A: Yes.

Q: That faulty wiring could have caused the fire, isn't that right?

A: It could have, but the result of all my investigation was that the fire was caused by arson.

(Pause 5)

Q: Fire Marshal Grant, you referred to Jane Byrne's book, *Fire Investigation*, on direct examination, didn't you?

A: Yes.

Q: Ms. Byrne has a Ph.D. in chemistry, doesn't she?

A: Yes.

Q: And she's the chair of the Chemistry Department at City University, isn't she?

A: Yes.

Q: She's written over a hundred articles on fire investigations, hasn't she?

A: Yes.

Q.   In fact she wrote the book which you referred to as 'the bible,' didn't she?

A: Yes.

Q.   You've attended conferences where Dr. Byrne was the primary instructor, haven't you?

A.   Yes, many times.

Q: Now Fire Marshal Grant, despite your qualifications, you wouldn't consider yourself as eminent an authority on fire investigations as Dr. Byrne, would you?

A: No, of course not.

Q: Let me show you Defendant's Exhibit 1 and refer you to chapter 1, section 1. Doesn't it say there that, 'The primary rule of fire investigation is that you should not reach the conclusion of arson unless and until you can rule out all accidental causes'?

Defense Attorney: Objection, Your Honor. We request a limiting instruction that the information be admitted for purposes of impeachment only and not for its truth.

(Pause 6)

A: Yes.

Q: Faulty wiring is an accidental cause, isn't it sir?

A: Yes.

Q: I have no further questions of this witness.

The defendant's lawyer asked the following questions on redirect examination.

Q: Did you prepare a report of your investigation of the Acme fire at 111 Main Street on February 10, 2004?

(Pause 7)

A: Yes, I'm required as part of my duties as a Fire Marshal to file a report of all my investigations. The law in this state requires that I make my report within five days of completing my investigation.

Q: Showing you what's been marked as Defendant's Exhibit 2 for identification, do you recognize it?

A: Yes, that's my report on the Acme fire.

Q: *Your Honor, I offer Defendant's Exhibit 2 for identification in evidence.*

Q2:   *We have no objection so long as the defendant's counsel will stipulate to the admissibility of the report of Dr. Morgan, whom the plaintiff will call as an expert witness during rebuttal.*

(Pause 8)

Vignette
17

Impeachment—Fed. R. Evid. 607–608, 611

Plaintiff Porter sues Defendant Stevenson for personal injuries growing out of a barroom fight. In his case in chief, Porter called an eyewitness, Wills, who testified that the defendant struck the plaintiff in an unprovoked attack. Defendant's lawyer is now cross-examining Wilson.

Q: Mr. Wills, it's true, isn't it, that you knew the defendant Davies before the barroom altercation?

A: I guess I had run into him once or twice before.

Q: In fact, Mr. Wills, hadn't you attacked Mr. Stevenson in a fist fight approximately one year ago?

Objection—this is a prior bad act which does not go to truth and veracity.

(Pause 1)

Vignette
18

Impeachment—Fed. R. Evid. 607–608, 611

Bob Petry, the plaintiff, sues the defendant, James Vitale, for personal injuries arising from an automobile collision. After the plaintiff testified that the defendant ran a red light causing the collision and his injuries, the plaintiff rested his case. The defendant called Jack Smith, a passenger who was in his car at the time of the collision. Smith testified that the plaintiff rather than the defendant ran a red light, causing the accident. We pick up in the midst of the plaintiff's cross-examination of Smith.

Q: Mr. Smith, you knew the defendant, Mr. Vitale, before the automobile collision involved in this case, didn't you?

A: Yes.

Q: And you had worked for him for three years before the accident hadn't you?

A: That's right.

Q: And about two weeks after the collision in this case, you had an argument with the defendant because you were drinking beer on the job?

Objection—irrelevant.

Q: *Your Honor, we'll connect this up in one or two more questions.*

(Pause 1)

Judge: *The witness will answer the question.*

A: Yes.

Q: It's true, isn't it Mr. Smith, that your boss, Mr. Vitale, the defendant in this case, told you that he wouldn't fire you for drinking on the job if you testified that the collision in this case was the plaintiff's fault?

(Pause 2)

Vignette

19

Impeachment (Prior Convictions)—Fed. R. Evid. 607–608, 611

David Hodkins, the plaintiff, has sued Business Machines Incorporated (BMI) claiming that he was fired from his job because of his age. The plaintiff was fifty years old at the time he was fired. The plaintiff calls Mary Lauvenson, an employment counselor, to testify as to his damages. We pick up in the midst of the cross-examination of Lauvenson by the defendant's counsel.

Q: Isn't it true that you were once employed by RCA in their Research and Development Department?

A: Yes, many years ago.

Q: Actually, just four years ago wasn't it?

A: I guess so.

Q: And weren't you fired by RCA for stealing and selling trade secrets?

(Pause 1)

A: No.

Q: Let me show you Plaintiff's Exhibit #42 for identification. That's a letter you received from David Cartwright, the President of RCA, informing you that you were fired for stealing and selling RCA's trade secrets, isn't it?

(Pause 2)

Q: Isn't it correct that you got caught at RCA because James Wheller of BMI informed RCA that you had attempted to sell RCA's trade secrets to BMI?

(Pause 3)

Vignette

20

Impeachment—Fed. R. Evid. 607–608, 611

James Butler sues Don Green for assault and battery growing out of bar fight. Green claims self-defense. Jane Davis, a witness to the fight, testified for the plaintiff that Green attacked Butler. The defense now cross-examines Ms. Davis.

Q: Ms. Davis, you knew the plaintiff before this matter arose, didn't you?

A: I guess so.

Q: In fact, you saw James Butler in another fight about six months earlier, didn't you?

Objection. Counsel can't impeach my client; he's not on the witness stand. Besides, this is a prior act which does not go to truthfulness. It's also prejudicial.

Q: *Your Honor, if you allow me a few more questions, the relevance and admissibility of this line of questioning will become apparent.*

Court: I'll allow a few more questions.

Q: Ms. Davis, you witnessed James Butler get into a fight about six months ago, didn't you?

A: Yes.

Q: That fight took place at Jimmy's Go-Go Bar & Grill didn't it?

A: That's right.

Q: And the fight happened because James Butler came to your defense when another man was annoying you, isn't that right?

I renew my objection, your Honor.

(Pause 1)

Vignette

21

Impeachment—Fed. R. Evid. 607–608, 611

Paula Price has sued Danielle Diaz for conversion of property. Price claims that when she left her ring for cleaning at Diaz' jewelry store it contained five high quality diamonds, but when it was returned the diamonds had been replaced with glass. Diaz claims that the stones were glass when Price brought in the ring.

Paula Price is the first witness for the plaintiff. We pick up in the midst of her direct examination.

Q: Ms. Price, after you concluded that Ms. Diaz switched the stones in your ring, did you ever talk to other people about her?

A: Yes. I sure wish I'd done it before I entrusted her with my diamonds.

Q: Did those people know Ms. Diaz?

A: Yes, they all said they'd had the bad judgment to have shopped at her store.

Q: Did any of those people ever talk about whether Ms. Diaz is a truthful person or not?

A: Yes.

Q: Among those people, what is Ms. Diaz' reputation for truthfulness?

(Pause 1)

Ms. Price concluded her direct testimony and there was no cross-examination. The plaintiff then called Gail Gibson. We pick up in the midst of Ms. Gibson's direct examination.

Q: Ms. Gibson, do you know the plaintiff, Paula Price?

A: Yes, we've been good friends since we were children.

Q: During the time that you have known her, have you formed an opinion about her character for truthfulness?

A: Yes, I have.

Q: What is that opinion?

(Pause 2)

Q: Do you know people who also know the defendant, Ms. Diaz?

A: Yes, I do.

Q: In what circumstances do these people know Ms. Diaz?

A: Most of them have shopped in her store.

Q: Among these people, does Ms. Diaz have a reputation for honesty?

A: Yes, she does.

Q: What is that reputation?

(Pause 3)

Ms. Gibson concluded her direct examination. We rejoin the trial at the beginning of her cross-examination by the defense.

Q: Ms. Gibson, you don't work, do you?

A: No, not right now.

Q: You used to work, though, didn't you?

A: Yes.

Q: Isn't it true you were fired from your last position as a cashier for stealing?

(Pause 4)

Q: Isn't it true that your former boss accused you of stealing from the cash register?

(Pause 5)

Q: And you in fact did steal from your employer's cash register, didn't you?

(Pause 6)

A: No, I did not.

Q: No further questions.

This concluded the cross-examination of Ms. Gibson. Her redirect examination by the plaintiff's attorney follows.

Q: Why is it that you are no longer working?

A: I've applied to return to school, to finish my degree. I'm fortunate enough that my family can support me while I finish my education.

Q: Getting back to the case at hand, had you ever seen Ms. Price's ring before she left it for cleaning at the defendant's jewelry store?

(Pause 7)

The plaintiff concluded her case and rested. The defense called as its first witness the defendant, Danielle Diaz. We pick up in the midst of Ms. Diaz' direct examination.

Q: Ms. Diaz, do you know people who know the plaintiff, Paula Price?

A: Yes, I do. Lots of my customers are friends and business associates of hers.

Q: Among those people, does Ms. Price have a reputation for truthfulness?

A: Yes, I've heard people talk about her on many occasions.

Q: What is that reputation?

(Pause 8)

A: She has a reputation as being a chronic liar.

Q: Do you know Gail Gibson?

A: Yes, we used to work at the same place. Neither of us works there anymore.

Q: Why doesn't Ms. Gibson work there anymore?

(Pause 9)

Vignette

22

Impeachment (Prior Convictions)—Fed. R. Evid. 609

Raymond Dawson is a criminal defendant on trial for Vehicular Homicide arising from his allegedly reckless driving of an automobile on January 1, 2004. The government's first witness, Ben Wilson, testified on direct as an eyewitness to Dawson's erratic driving at the time of the collision with the victim, who was a pedestrian.

On cross-examination, defense counsel asks the following questions:

Q: Are you the same Ben Wilson convicted of assault and battery in Iowa three years ago for which you received an eighteen-month prison sentence?

(Pause 1)

A: Yes.

Q: Weren't you also convicted of misdemeanor assault in Minnesota in 2003?

(Pause 2)

A: Yes.

Q: Didn't you also plead guilty in Minnesota in 1998 for fraud for which you received a suspended sentence?

(Pause 3)

A: Yes.

Q: Nothing further.

The defense calls the defendant Raymond Dawson to testify in his own behalf. Dawson denied driving recklessly on the night the victim died, and claimed that the victim caused the accident by running out in front of his car. On cross-examination, the government asked the following questions.

Q: Are you the same Raymond Dawson who was convicted in this state in 1996 of rape for which you received a sentence of four years in prison?

(Pause 4)

A: Yes.

Q: Weren't you also arrested for possession of stolen property just four weeks ago in this state?

(Pause 5)

A: Yes.

Q: Weren't you convicted of the misdemeanor of passing bad checks in this state in 2001 for which you received a sentence of probation?

(Pause 6)

A: Yes.

Q: Weren't you also convicted of perjury in this state in 1991, receiving a two-year sentence?

(Pause 7)

A: Yes.

Q: Now finally, Mr. Dawson, weren't you convicted of vehicular homicide and driving under the influence of alcohol in this state only last year, for which you received a three-year suspended sentence?

(Pause 8)

A: No.

Dan Johnson, a passenger in Dawson's car at the time of the accident was called by the defense and testified consistently with the defendant that the victim ran out in front of Dawson's car. On cross-examination, Johnson was questioned only about his two-year-old prior conviction for perjury, which he denied. After Johnson was excused, the defendant rested and the following occurred.

Q: (*Government's counsel:*) *Your Honor, by way of rebuttal I offer as Defendant's Exhibit 1, a certified copy of Dan Johnson's perjury conviction, and I would like the court's permission to publish it to the jury.*

(Pause 9)

Q: I now call Walter Winston to the stand as a rebuttal witness.

Q: Please state your name and address for the record.

A: Walt Winston, 533 Commonwealth Avenue in the city.

Q: What is your occupation, Mr. Winston?

A: I'm a bartender at Jonny's Bar and Grill in the city.

Q: Do you know Dan Johnson?

A: Yeah, he comes in and drinks at my bar about twice a week.

Q: Directing your attention to January 2, 2004, were you working that day?

A: I was, from 4 P.M. to midnight.

Q: Did you see Johnson on January 2?

A: Yes, I definitely remember him coming into the bar and talking about his car accident on New Year's Day.

Q: What did he say?

A: He said that he and the plaintiff were in an accident on New Year's Day. He also said that Dawson been drinking on New Year's Day and had run a stop sign, and struck and killed the victim who was crossing the street in the crosswalk.

(Pause 10)

Vignette

23

Impeachment (Prior Convictions)—Fed. R. Evid. 609

Plaintiff Judith Pratt brings a medical malpractice action against the defendant, Dr. Richard Denton, claiming that Dr. Denton negligently performed surgery upon the plaintiff, causing her permanent disability. After Pratt testified on direct examination, the defendant's attorney began cross-examination.

Q: Are you the same Judith Pratt who was convicted of armed robbery in Pennsylvania in 1999, for which you were sentenced to three years in prison?

Objection, irrelevant and prejudicial.

(Pause 1)

A: Yes.

Q: Are you the same Judith Pratt who was arrested for embezzlement just six months ago?

Objection, irrelevant and prejudicial.

(Pause 2)

Q: Are you the same Judith Pratt convicted of misdemeanor assault in New Jersey in 2003?

Objection.

(Pause 3)

Q: Were you convicted of welfare fraud in 1997 for which you received a suspended sentence?

Objection.

(Pause 4)

A: Yes.

Q: Weren't you convicted in this state for perjury in 1994?

Objection, irrelevant.

(Pause 5)

Q: Aren't you the same Judith Pratt who was indicted only two weeks ago for falsely failing to report income tax for the 1999 tax year?

Objection, it's not a conviction.

(Pause 6)

Court:Sustained.

Q: Didn't you knowingly fail to report all of your income for 1999?

A: No.

Q: Showing you what's been marked as Defendant's Exhibit 2 for identification, isn't this your 1999 tax return?

Objection.

(Pause 7)

Vignette

24

Impeachment and Rehabilitation—Fed. R. Evid. 613, 801(d)(1)(B)

Wayne Walker was waiting for a bus on the corner of Main Street and Kennedy Boulevard when two cars collided in the intersection. A lawsuit was filed with the plaintiff claiming that the defendant drove through a red light. The plaintiff's car, a Mercedes Benz, had been traveling northbound. The defendant's car, a Toyota, had been traveling westbound.

At the trial, the plaintiff testified and then called Walker to testify. Walker testified on direct examination that at the time of the collision the plaintiff driving the Mercedes had the green light. We pick up in the midst of Walker's cross-examination.

Q: Mr. Walker, this is not the first time you have answered questions about this accident, is it?

A: No.

Q: In fact, the very day after the accident, someone came to your house and asked you questions, isn't that right?

A: Yeah, that's right.

Q: And you answered those questions, didn't you?

A: Yeah, I suppose so. I mean it wasn't formal questions like here in court, but I did tell the guy what I had seen.

Q: Your Honor, I have here a document previously marked Defendant's Exhibit A for identification. It is the statement of Mr. Walker given the day after the accident. I offer Defendant's Exhibit A in evidence.

(Pause 1)

Q: Mr. Walker, isn't it true that on the day after the accident you told the investigator who came to your house that at the time of the collision the traffic light was green for the westbound traffic?

A: No, I didn't say that.

Q: Mr. Walker, please take a look at Defendant's Exhibit A for identification.

A: Okay, I've looked at it.

Q: That's your signature at the bottom of this document, isn't it?

A: Yeah, I signed it.

Q: And this is the document that the investigator filled out after he asked you questions about the collision, isn't it?

A: Yeah.

Q: I'm going to read from this Defendant's Exhibit A, and I want you to tell me if I'm reading it correctly. Doesn't Defendant's Exhibit A say, "At the time of the collision, the traffic light was green for the westbound traffic?"

A: Yeah.

Q: And those words were on the page before you signed you name, weren't they?

A: Yeah, I suppose.

Q: Your Honor, I again offer Defendant's Exhibit A in evidence.

(Pause 2)

Mr. Walker also admitted during cross-examination that three weeks prior to trial he had dinner with the plaintiff's lawyer at La Bon Vie, the city's most expensive and exclusive French restaurant. We rejoin the trial in the midst of the plaintiff's redirect examination of Mr. Walker.

Q: Mr. Walker, when was the next time immediately before today that you and I spoke?

A: Yesterday, in your partner's office.

Q: What did we talk about?

A: What I could expect today.

Q: Did we talk about the collision?

A: Yeah, of course.

Q: What did you say about who had the green light at the time of the collision?

(Pause 3)

Q: Mr. Walker, I'd like you to think back to the first time we met. Where was that?

A: In your office.

Q: And when was that?

A: About a week after the collision.

Q: How did you come to be in my office?

A: You asked me to come and make a formal statement of what I saw.

Q: Who was present?

A: You, me, and one of those stenographer people.

Q: What did you say about who had the green light at the time of the collision?

(Pause 4)

A: I told you that the Mercedes had the green light.

Vignette

25

Impeachment—Fed. R. Evid. 613

BMI sues Minicom in a contract action involving computer parts. The defendant, Minicom's Vice-President for Purchasing, Michael Lubell, has testified on direct examination. We pick up in the midst of the cross-examination of Michael Lubell. Refer to vignette 56 for the factual background of this Vignette.

Q: Now Mr. Lubell, you testified on direct that you held four jobs prior to coming to Minicom, including a job as a computer programmer, isn't that correct?

A: Yes, that's right.

Q: Do you remember coming to my office for a deposition July 12, 2003?

A: Yes, I guess so.

Q: Your lawyer, Mr. Richards, was there wasn't he?

A: Yeah.

Q: You were under oath weren't you?

A: Yes.

Q: I asked you some questions and you gave answers, isn't that right?

A: Yes.

Q: I'm showing you a document marked as Plaintiff's Exhibit 22 for identification. That's your deposition, isn't it?

A: Yes.

Q: Directing your attention to page 8 of Exhibit 22, didn't I ask you the following questions and didn't you give the following answers: Question: 'What jobs have you held before coming to Minicom? Answer: Shoe salesman, jeans shop operator, tie salesman. Question: Mr. Lubell, what other jobs have you had? Answer: None.'

Objection—beyond the scope of direct and irrelevant.

(Pause 1)

Vignette

26

Impeachment—Fed. R. Evid. 613

Kenneth Brown has sued Robert Byrd for personal injuries arising out of an automobile collision that occurred on November 1, 2003. Brown claims that he received severe back injuries when his car was rear-ended by Byrd while Brown was stopped at a stop sign. Defendant Byrd admits liability but contests Brown's damage claim. Specifically, it is the defendant's position that Brown is faking his back injuries.

During his direct examination, plaintiff Brown testified that one of the activities that he misses most is the ability to play tennis. He testified that he was a college tennis player and that since graduation, much of his social life centered around his tennis club. He further stated that playing tennis was a way to entertain business clients and that his inability to play tennis has damaged his earning capacity as a stockbroker. The direct testimony of Brown has concluded and we pick up in the midst of the cross-examination of Brown by defense counsel.

Q: On direct examination you claimed that your injuries from this accident have precluded you from playing tennis?

A: That's right.

Q: And that the inability to play tennis has hurt your social life?

A: That's right.

Q: You've never made that claim before today have you, sir?

A: I'm sure I have. It's true.

Q: Now Mr. Brown, this isn't the first time you've given sworn testimony regarding your claimed injuries and damages, is it?

A: No, I gave a . . . deposition?

Q: That's right. And at that deposition I was there, your lawyer was there, and a court reporter just like Mr. Jennings, just below you, was there to take down everything you said?

A: True.

Q: I asked you questions, you answered, and your lawyer had an opportunity to ask questions as well?

A: Yes, but my lawyer didn't ask me anything that day.

Q: Before I asked any questions you took an oath to tell the truth, didn't you?

A: Yes.

Q: You swore to tell the truth, the whole truth, and nothing but the truth, right?

A: Yes.

Q: And I told you I was interested in finding out about everything that happened to you in the car accident and all the damages that you claimed resulted from it, didn't I?

A: Yes, something like that.

Q: And I asked you to give full and complete answers to my questions?

A: You did.

Q: You agreed to give full and complete answers as well?

A: I did.

Q: I told you that if during the deposition you remembered something that would make an earlier answer more complete or accurate, you should feel free to tell me about it?

A: That's right.

Q: And after each break I asked if you had anything to add to previous answers you had given?

A: You did.

Q: And you never once took the opportunity during the deposition to supplement your answers, did you?

A: There was no reason to.

Q: And after the deposition was over, you received a word-processed transcript of my questions and your answers, didn't you?

A: That's right.

Q: You were asked to read and correct and supplement, if necessary, any of your answers?

A: That's right.

Q: You read and signed your deposition?

A: I did.

Q: Yet you made no corrections or additions to your answers did you?

A: No, I didn't. No additions or corrections were necessary.

Q: Showing you Exhibit 29, that's your signed deposition isn't it?

A: Yes, it is.

Q: Now again, sir, you claim that your social life has been interfered with because of your inability to play tennis?

A: That's true. It has.

Q: Well in your deposition we discussed the effects of your injury on your personal life, didn't we?

A: I believe so.

Q: Please turn to page 110 of your deposition, beginning at line 4 and read along with me to make sure I read this correctly. Your deposition states:

   Question: Do you claim any damages from your injuries to your personal life?

   Answer: My back hurts me a lot so I don't go out as often as I used to.

   Question: What other claims do you make?

   Answer: This is a little embarrassing but I can't perform sexually as well as I used to because of the pain in my back and loss of flexibility.

   Question: What else?

   Answer: My recreational activities are limited.

   Question: How so?

   Answer: I used to be a lot more active. I'm a lot more sedentary than I used to be.

   Question: What other claims of damage to your personal life do you make?

   Answer: That's it, I guess.

Q: Have I read your deposition correctly?

A: Yes you have.

Q: Those were the questions I asked and those were the answers you gave, weren't they?

A: Yes, that's what it says.

Q: And you never once supplemented your answers did you?

A: No.

Q:
So today in court is the first time that you've claimed damage because of an ability to play tennis, isn't it?

A: I did say my recreation was limited.

Q: But there was no mention of tennis playing, right?

A: That's right.

(Pause 1)

Q: And no mention of your tennis club?

A: Right again. At least not there.

Q: Turn to the back of your deposition will you, Sir?

A: I have.

Q: Do you see the first appendix that has a key as to words you used in your deposition?

A: I do.

Q: They are listed alphabetically in an index, aren't they sir?

A: Yes.

Q: Go to the T's and when you get to the word 'tennis' read it to the jury and tell us the page on which you used the word 'tennis' so we can see what you've said.

Witness reads to self and looks up.)

Q: At least according to that index, you never used the word 'tennis' in over 380 pages of transcript, did you?

A: I guess not.

(Pause 2)

Vignette

27

Impeachment and Rehabilitation (Prior Inconsistent and Consistent Statements), Rule of Completeness, Relevance—Fed. R. Evid. 613, 801(d)(1)(A), 801(d)(1)(B), 407–411

Mark Berman, the plaintiff, has sued John Hunter, the defendant, for personal injuries that he sustained resulting from a car accident. The plaintiff has called Norman Harrison as a witness. Harrison testified that while driving, the defendant, Hunter, ran a red light and collided with the plaintiff's car. Before cross-examination begins, the defendant marks Harrison's deposition as Defendant's Exhibit 1 for identification and marks a statement allegedly made by Harrison to the defendant's insurance investigator, Ray Noll, as Defendant's Exhibit 2 for identification. The cross-examination of Harrison begins.

Q: This accident happened on June 1, 2003, didn't it?

A: Yes, at 3 P.M.

Q: The police investigated the accident, didn't they?

A: Yes.

Q: You gave them your name and address?

A: Yes.

Q: On June 5, 2003 you were visited at your home by Ray Noll weren't you?

A: Yes, he came to my home.

Q: He told you he was investigating the accident of June 1, didn't he?

A: Yes.

Q: You told Mr. Noll that you didn't see the accident happen, didn't you?

A: No, that's not true.

Q: Didn't you give him a signed statement to that effect?

A: No.

Q: Let me show you Defendant's Exhibit 2 for identification and direct your attention to the lower right hand corner; that's your signature, isn't it?

A: No, it's not.

Q: Defendant's Exhibit 2 for identification isn't your statement?

A: No, it's not.

Q: You didn't write and sign Defendant's Exhibit 2 for identification saying that you didn't see the accident?

(Pause 1)

Q: You did give a deposition concerning this accident on October 15, 2003, didn't you?

A: Yes.

Q: At that time you were under oath?

A: Yes.

Q: After you answered both my questions and the questions of the defendant's lawyer, those questions and answers were typed up, weren't they?

A: Yes.

Q: You read over your deposition and signed it, didn't you?

A: Yes.

Q: Showing you what's been marked as Defendant's Exhibit 1 for identification and directing your attention to the last page, that's your signature, isn't it?

A: Yes, this is my deposition.

Q: Directing your attention to page 22, line 8, I asked you how the accident happened, didn't I?

A: Yes, you did.

Q: You responded, 'I'm not really sure, but I think that the defendant ran the red light,' didn't you?

A: Yes, but on reflection I am sure.

Your Honor, I ask that the jury be instructed that the deposition statement of Mr. Harrison not be considered for the truth of the matter asserted but only as a prior inconsistent statement.

(Pause 2)

The defendant had no further questions on cross-examination and the plaintiff's lawyer asked the following questions on redirect examination of the Mr. Harrison.

Q: At the time of your deposition did I ask you any questions?

A: Yes, after the defendant's lawyer.

Q: Directing your attention to page 52, line 6 of Defendant's Exhibit 1 for identification, please read the question and answer to the jury.

A: Sure, it says here, 'Question: 'You told the defendant's lawyer that you weren't sure how the accident happened, what did you mean by that?' Answer: 'I'm not sure exactly what part of the defendant's car hit the plaintiff's car, but I am sure that the defendant ran the red light.'

(Pause 3)

Q: Directing your attention to June 10, 2003 at 5 P.M. where were you?

A: At your office to talk to you about the accident.

Q: Did I ask you how the accident happened?

A: Yes, I told you that the defendant ran the red light.

(Pause 4)

The plaintiff then testified as to his version of the accident, stating that the defendant ran the red light. The plaintiff also testified as to his injuries. After the defendant cross-examined the plaintiff, the plaintiff rested. The defendant calls as his first witness, Ray Noll. The direct examination follows.

Q: What is your name and occupation?

A: Ray Noll, I'm an accident investigator.

Q: Were you working on June 5, 2003?

A: Yes, I was investigating the accident between the plaintiff and the defendant.

Q: What did you do?

A: I obtained the copy of the police report of the accident and went to the home of one of the witnesses listed on the report, Norman Harrison.

Q: Was Mr. Harrison at home?

A: Yes, we talked briefly about the accident.

Q: What did he tell you?

A: He told me that he didn't see the accident.

(Pause 5)

Q: What did you do after talking with Mr. Harrison?

A: I asked him if he would write out a statement that said what he told me.

Q: Did he do that?

A: Well, he said he was busy so I asked him if I could leave my standard statement form for him to fill out so I could pick it up the next day. He agreed and I picked up the statement form from his spouse the next day.

Q: Showing you what's been marked as Defendant's Exhibit 2, for identification, do you recognize it?

A: Yes, it's the statement of Harrison that I picked up on June 6, 2003.

Q: Is Defendant's Exhibit 2 for identification in the same condition as when you received it from Mr. Harrison?

A: Yes, except I put my initials with the date on it when I picked it up.

Q: Your Honor, I offer Defendant's Exhibit 2 for identification into evidence.

(Pause 6)

This concludes the direct examination of Mr. Noll. The cross-examination by the plaintiff follows.

Q: You are not an independent investigator, are you Sir?

A: No.

Q: In fact you work for the Acme Insurance Company don't you?

A: That's right.

Q: You were working for Acme in June 2003, weren't you?

A: Yes.

Q: Acme had a policy on the defendant, John Hunter in June, 2003, didn't they?

Objection and I move for a mistrial.

(Pause 7)

Q: After this accident, you know that Mr. Hunter, the defendant, was dropped as an insured by Acme, don't you?

Objection and I move for a mistrial.

(Pause 8)

Q: You met with my client, Mark Berman, on June 8, 2003 didn't you?

A: Yes.

Q: You saw him at the Memorial Hospital didn't you?

A: Yes.

Q: At that time didn't you tell the plaintiff, Mr. Berman, that you had talked to the witness, Mr. Harrison?

A: Yes.

Q: Didn't you tell my client that in light of what Harrison said, that you would write him a check, on the spot, for $15,000 and agree to pay all his medical bills if my client would sign a release?

(Pause 9)

Vignette

28

Relevance—Fed. R. Evid. 401–402

Defendant Charles Rogers, a City police officer, has been charged with a murder committed while he was off duty. The victim was shot dead-center in the heart. The defendant, Rogers, claims that he fired his gun accidentally while struggling with the victim who was the first aggressor.

The prosecutor calls the City Chief of Police as a witness.

Q: What is your name and occupation?

A: Joan Simmons, City Chief of Police.

Q: Do you know the defendant?

A: Yes, he's been on my force for seven years.

Q: What are his duties?

A: For the past two years he has been an instructor at our shooting range. He shows our new recruits how to accurately shoot at human silhouette targets. He does a good job.

Q: How was the defendant trained to shoot?

A: In the same way he now teaches the others.

Q: Is he a good shot?

A: He's an expert—the best we have.

Q: I see. When shooting at the silhouette, how does one obtain the maximum score?

A: It's done by hitting a circle drawn around the heart of the target.

(Pause 1)

Vignette

29

Relevance—Fed. R. Evid. 401–402

The defendant, Robert Ryan, is charged with murdering his wife after hearing that she was leaving him for another man. His defense is insanity, disassociative reaction, which is characterized by amnesia regarding the traumatic events.

On cross-examination of the defendant, the prosecution asks the following:

Q: Are you familiar with the book *Anatomy of a Murder*?

A: Yes, slightly.

Q: Have you read it?

A: I may have skimmed it.

Q: When was this?

A: It was a few weeks before my wife died.

Q: You recall, don't you, that in the book the defense asserted by the jealous husband charged with killing his wife was "disassociative reaction" which made him amnesiac?

A: I don't remember.

(Pause 1)

On rebuttal the prosecutor calls the defendant's daughter as a witness. We pick up in the midst of the direct examination of Sarah Ryan by the prosecuting attorney.

Q: Are you familiar with the book *Anatomy of a Murder*?

A: Yes.

Q: Have you ever seen it in your parents' house?

A: Yes I did—two weeks before the murder.

Q: Did you ever see anyone in the house reading this book?

A: Yes, my father.

Q: When did you first notice your father reading the book?

A: About two weeks before the murder.

Q: Did you ever see a bookmark in the book?

A: Yes, it was about two-thirds of the way into the book when I first saw my father reading it.

Q: And when did you last see him reading this book?

A: It would have been a week before the murder.

Q: Was there a bookmark in the book?

A: Yes.

Q: Where, at this time was the bookmark placed?

A: It was about a fourth of the way through.

(Pause 2)

Vignette

30

Relevance—Fed. R. Evid. 401–402

Rick Jackson, an air conditioning mechanic, is charged with importation and possession of marijuana. On May 1, 2003, Jackson and his wife arrived at Kennedy Airport in New York from Istanbul, Turkey. Customs officers found four pounds of marijuana in Jackson's baggage.

Jackson asserts that he is innocent. He claims that after September 11, 2001, air travellers are discouraged from locking their luggage. He claims that his luggage was not locked and that someone put the marijuana into his baggage with the intention of recovering it after the customs checkpoint. In effect, Jackson claims he was an unwitting courier. He further claims that he and his wife were in Turkey as part of their lifetime dream: a second honeymoon.

The prosecution calls the police officer who made the initial arrest.

Q: Please state your name.

A: My name is Edna Hermann.

Q: Ms. Hermann, what is your occupation?

A: I have been a police officer for fifteen years.

Q: Officer Hermann, were you working on May 1, 2003?

A: Yes, I was.

Q: What happened on May 1?

A: I arrested the defendant on a narcotics charge in response to a call from the customs officers at Kennedy Airport.

Q: After arresting the defendant, what did you do?

A: I read the defendant his rights.

Q: Did you search the defendant?

A: Yes.

Q: Did you find anything?

A: Yes.

Q: What did you find?

A: The only thing he had in his pockets was a business card; you know, the kind they carry in wallets.

Q: Officer, showing you a card previously marked as Government's Exhibit #1 for identification, can you identify it?

A: Yes. It's the card I seized from the defendant.

Q: Your Honor, I offer this card as Government's Exhibit 1 and ask that the witness read it to the jury.

(Pause 1)

A: The card says 'Janet Samuels, Esq., 10 Court Street, N.Y., N.Y., phone number (555) 337-8707.'

(Pause 2)

Q: Do you know Ms. Samuels?

A: Yes. She is an attorney in Manhattan who specializes in criminal defense litigation—particularly drug cases.

Vignette

31

Character Evidence—Fed. R. Evid. 404(a)

The parents of Paul Peters, a seven-year-old child, bring an action against Doris Drake, a school bus driver, and the school district, to recover damages for injuries Peters suffered when the school bus crashed into a utility pole. The theory of the claim against Drake is negligence. The theory against the school district is negligence in hiring and entrusting the bus to Drake.

At trial, the plaintiffs call Richard Spock as a witness.

Q: Mr. Spock, what do you do for a living?

A: I am a retired supervisor of school bus drivers for a school district in the western part of the state.

Q: Do you know Doris Drake, the defendant in this case?

A: Yes.

Q: How do you know her?

A: I fired Ms. Drake as a school bus driver in my district.

Q: How long ago?

A: Approximately four years ago. I fired her because she had been involved in two accidents where no other vehicles were involved.

(By Drake's attorney) *Objection, this is inadmissible against my client.*

(Pause 1)

Vignette

32

Character Evidence—Fed. R. Evid. 404(a)

The defendant, Harold Richardson, has been charged with the assault of Ron Reynolds. Richardson calls his neighbor, Robin Bartel, as his first witness. We pick up in the midst of Bartel's direct examination.

Q: Mr. Bartel, how long have you known the defendant, Harold Richardson?

A: About twelve years.

Q: How do you know him?

A: We have worked together for those twelve years at General Manufacturing Company in Doylestown.

Q: Mr. Bartel, where does Harold Richardson live?

A: Jenkintown.

Q: And do you know Mr. Richardson's reputation for truthfulness in Jenkintown?

A: I do.

Q: What is that reputation?

(Pause 1)

A: He is known as a truthful man.

Q: Mr. Bartel, do you have an opinion as to Harold Richardson's character for peacefulness?

A: Yes.

Q: What is that opinion?

A: He is a peaceful, gentle, man.

(Pause 2)

Q: Can you cite any instance where Mr. Richardson demonstrated his peacefulness?

(Pause 3)

The plaintiff now is cross-examining Bartel.

Q: Mr. Bartel, have you heard that the defendant Richardson beat up a woman named Jane Adams in Pennsylvania in 2001 in a bar fight?

Objection—prejudicial and the plaintiff is using specific instances of conduct to impeach.

(Pause 4)

Vignette

33

Character Evidence—Fed. R. Evid. 404(a), 608

Darlene Darrow is on trial for the aggravated assault of Vicki Voight. Voight's recovery from injuries Darrow is charged with inflicting on her in the assault, was not sufficient to enable Voight to be called as a witness. In her opening statement, Defense Counsel stated that Voight had assaulted Darrow with a knife and thus she would prove that Darrow had acted in self-defense when she struck Voight with a baseball bat. The prosecution called as its first witness Fred Frank—a friend of the victim and an eyewitness to the assault. We pick up in the midst of Frank's direct examination.

Q: Mr. Frank, how well did you know the victim at the time of altercation?

A: Oh, gee, really well. We lived next door to each other all our lives and attended the same college. She had been dating my roommate for the two years before the fight. So, to answer to your question, I'd say that at the time of the fight we had been close friends for twenty years or more.

Q: Do you have an opinion about Ms. Voight's character for peacefulness at the time of the altercation?

A: Yes, I do.

Q: What is that opinion?

(Pause 1)

A: She was a very peaceful person.

Q: Mr. Frank, did you know the defendant before the date of the altercation?

A: Yes, I did.

Q: For how long?

A: For about three years. We worked together and bowled in the same league.

Q: Had you formed an opinion about the defendant's character for peacefulness or violence, and again I want to you to address your answer to the time of the altercation.

A: Yes, I had.

Q: What was that opinion?

(Pause 2)

A: That she is a violent woman.

The prosecution put on the remainder of its case and then rested. The defense began its case by calling the defendant. We pick up in the midst of the defendant's direct examination.

Q: Ms. Darrow, for how long had you known Vicki Voight before the night you and she got into an altercation?

A: I had known her for about three years. She was real good friends with Fred, and I worked with Fred. We socialized in the same circles a lot on weekends.

Q: At the time of the altercation, had you formed an opinion about Ms. Voight's character for truthfulness and honesty?

A: Yes, I had.

Q: What was that opinion?

(Pause 3)

A: You couldn't depend on anything she said.

Q: Ms. Darrow, besides Mr. Frank, did you know other people who knew Ms. Voight?

A: Yeah, sure. Like I said, we ran in the same circles on weekends.

Q: Among the people you know, did you ever hear anyone discuss Ms. Voight with regard to how she interacts with people, that is, do you know her reputation for violence?

A: I sure did. Lots of people talked about her. She's got some reputation.

Q: What is that reputation?

(Pause 4)

A: For as long as I'd known her, she was aggressive and violent.

(Pause 5)

The defendant concluded her direct testimony. We pick up in the midst of her cross-examination.

Q: Ms. Darrow, isn't it true that just three months before the altercation with Ms.Voight you were involved in a bar fight with another patron of the bar?

(Pause 6)

The defense put on the remainder of its case and rested. On rebuttal, the prosecution called Robert Richardson. We pick up in the midst of Richardson's direct examination.

Q: Mr. Richardson, how long have you known Ms. Voight?

A: I've known Vicki for four years. We work together.

Q: Do you have an opinion about Ms. Voight's character for peacefulness?

A: I sure do. I remember in particular an incident that really solidified my opinion of her.

Q: Please tell us what happened.

(Pause 7)

Q: Do you know people who know the defendant, Ms. Darrow?

A: Yes, I do.

Q: Have those people ever discussed Ms. Darrow's reputation?

A: Yes, they have.

Q: What is Ms. Darrow's reputation for being a violent person?

(Pause 8. Assume the witness will testify that Ms. Darrow has a reputation for being a violent individual).

Vignette

34

Character—Fed. R. Evid. 404(b)

The Estate of John Haynes brings a wrongful-death action against Diane Doaks, arising from a hit-and-run incident on August 11, 2003 at 2;30 P.M. when Doaks is alleged to have killed Haynes, a pedestrian, while operating a motor vehicle. The vehicle involved was a brown Mercedes with Pennsylvania tag number "ADH-418." Doaks does not own such a car. Haynes' estate calls Sergeant Wilson of the Pittsburgh Police Department. We pick up in the midst of Sergeant Wilson's testimony.

Q: Sergeant Wilson, do you know Ms. Doaks, the defendant?

A: Yes.

Q: When did you first see her?

A: Well, my partner and I were seated in a car in plainclothes in a parking garage in downtown Pittsburgh on August 11, 2003 at 4 A.M. We saw Ms. Doaks break into, and steal, a brown Mercedes 450 SL with the Pennsylvania tag 'ADH-418.'

Objection—irrelevant and a prior bad act.

(Pause 1)

Vignette

35

Character—Fed. R. Evid. 404(b)

At the trial of Ronald Davis for armed robbery while masked, committed on August 6, 2003, the government calls as a witness, Sam Walters, an owner of a firearms retail store. The government has earlier introduced a gun that was allegedly used in the robbery.

We pick up in the midst of Walters's testimony.

Q: Mr. Walters, showing you Government's Exhibit 1 for identification, I ask you to inspect it. Can you identify it?

A: (After looking at it) Yes, it is a .22 caliber pistol stolen from my store on August 1, 2003 of last year.

Q: How do you know?

A: Because the gun bears the serial number of the stolen gun.

Q: What happened in the robbery of the gun from your store on August 1 of last year?

Objection, irrelevant.

Q: *Your Honor, we'll connect this up in a very few questions.*

(Pause 1)

Judge: He may answer.

A: Yes. A man entered my store at about 10:30 A.M. on August 1, brandished a knife and took this gun from a glass case in front of me.

Q: Do you see that man in court today?

A: Yes, over there—the defendant.

Objection—this is a prior bad act offered on propensity. It's prejudicial.

(Pause 2)

Vignette

37

Character—Fed. R. Evid. 404(b)

The defendant, John Maxwell, is charged with fraud in making a false claim for damages against the local transit authority by filing a claim for a subway accident in which he was not involved.

At trial, the government offers the testimony of the claims supervisor for the transit authority. We pick up in the midst of the claims supervisor's testimony.

Q: Do you know the defendant in this case, John Maxwell?

A: Yes, I know who he is.

Q: How do you know Mr. Maxwell?

A: He has made many claims against the transit authority before.

Move to strike the answer.

(Pause 1)

Q: How many other claims has he made?

A: Six over the past ten years.

Q: What happened with those claims?

A: We tried every one of them and he lost each one after we proved he was not present at the time of any of those accidents.

(Pause 2)

Vignette

38

Character—Fed. R. Evid. 404(b)

Richards sues Davidson for fraud, alleging misrepresentation in the sale of vacationland in Louisiana. The fraud involves the use of falsified photographs that misled Richards as to the nature of the land that Davidson sold him. The photographs show dry, well landscaped lots, which were actually marshland and ninety percent under water year round. Peterson calls Watson, the victim of an earlier alleged land fraud perpetrated by Davidson in Florida. We pick up in the midst of Watson's testimony.

Q: Mr. Watson, do you know the defendant, Richard Davidson?

A: Yes, I met him three years ago.

Q: How did you come to know him?

A: Davidson approached me about the sale of some vacationland in Florida.

Q: Did you talk with Davidson?

A: Yes, he offered to sell me ten acres of Florida land for $3,000 per acre and said the land was hilly and dry. He also showed me some pictures of what he said was the land.

Q: Do you have those pictures?

A: No, I threw them away last year.

Q: Can you describe the pictures?

A: Yes, they showed a green, hilly, dry area.

Q: Did you buy the land?

A: Yes.

Q: Did you ever visit it?

A: Yes.

Q: Describe what you saw?

A: It was flat, bottomland, which was mostly under water.

(Pause 1)

Vignette

39

Character—Fed. R. Evid. 405

Peters sues Davidson in a defamation action. Peters alleges that Davidson told a number of people that Peters was "dishonest." Peters called Jones as a character witness. Jones testified that he had known Peters for twenty years, and that Peters had a reputation as an honest man. We pick up in the midst of the cross-examination of Jones, the character witness.

Q: Mr. Jones, do you know that Mr. Peters was a party to a land-fraud scheme committed four years ago?

Objection—irrelevant, prior bad act.

(Pause 1)

Q: Mr. Jones, are you aware that Mr. Peters pled guilty to perjury some twelve years ago in Pennsylvania?

Objection—irrelevant and you can't impeach the plaintiff without a foundation on cross.

(Pause 2)

Q: Now you don't really believe that a person who perjures himself and defrauds people is 'very honest,' do you?

(Pause 3)

Vignette

40

Character—Fed. R. Evid. 404(a)

Ralph Diamond is on trial for murder. Diamond calls a character witness, the Reverend Thomas Nicholson. The direct examination of Reverend Nicholson follows.

Q: What is your name and occupation?

A: Tom Nicholson. I am a Methodist minister.

Q: Do you know Ralph Diamond, the defendant in this case?

A: Yes, I've known Ralph for fifteen years as a neighbor of mine.

Q: How often do you see Ralph Diamond?

A: Usually about once a month, around our apartment complex.

Q: Do you know how he spends most of his time?

A: He is rather reclusive, staying in his apartment. He does not work—he's on disability. His only real activity is to play pinochle with three other guys who come to his apartment.

Q: Do you know Mr. Diamond's reputation for peacefulness in the community?

A: Yes.

Q: What is it?

(Pause 1)

A: He is known as a peaceful, gentle man.

Vignette

41
Character—Fed. R. Evid. 405

This is a libel action brought by Brian Peters against James Donnelly. According to the complaint, Donnelly called Peters a "damned liar," in response to a question from a third party who asked Donnelly about Peters.

Defendant Donnelly calls James Johnson as a witness. We pick up in the midst of Johnson's testimony.

Q: Mr. Johnson, do you know Brian Peters, the plaintiff in this case?

A: Yes, I do.

Q: How do you know him?

A: I am the personnel director at Bergen Advertising where Mr. Peters worked up to a month ago and I interviewed and hired Peters for our art department.

Q: When you interviewed Peters, did he describe his educational background?

A: Yes. He said he was a graduate of the Rhode Island School of Design.

Q: Did you ever discuss Peters's college degree with him again?

A: Yes, after his six-month probationary period was over, he came to me and said he expected a negative evaluation from his supervisor who was dissatisfied with his skills. He then admitted he was a self-taught artist and had no formal training at RISD or anywhere.

(Pause 1)

Vignette

42

Character—Fed. R. Evid. 405

The defendant, Helen Hoover, a prominent public official, is on trial for using and possessing cocaine. In pretrial pleadings and in its opening statement, the defense placed its emphasis on a defense of entrapment. As its first witness, the prosecution calls Rex Ray, who cooperated with the government in its investigation of Hoover. We pick up in the midst of Ray's testimony.

Q: Mr. Ray, how long had you known Ms. Hoover before the day of her arrest?

A: For about three years; we met at a political function and became friends.

Q: What kinds of things did you do together?

A: In the beginning we would get together for an after work drink or dinner. Later we started doing drugs together.

Q: Objection, your Honor; I move to strike the last clause of the witness's answer. Unless and until Ms. Hoover testifies, she cannot be impeached with specific acts of conduct, and even then the acts must pertain to truthfulness or untruthfulness.

(Pause 1)

The prosecution completed its case and rested. As its first witness, the defense called the defendant, Helen Hoover. We pick up in the midst of Hoover's direct examination.

Q: Ms. Hoover, had you at any time before the night in question used any form of contraband drugs?

A: No, I never did. In fact, on several occasions people used drugs in my presence and even offered me some, but I always said no. Moreover, on a voluntary basis, I and everyone in my office participate in random urinalysis. I would have never done that if I used drugs.

Objection, your Honor, I move to strike everything following the statement, 'No, I never did.' Everything else is self-serving description and outside the bounds of any permissible prior act evidence.

(Pause 2)

The defendant concluded her direct examination. We join the trial in the midst of the defendant's cross-examination by the prosecution.

Q: Ms. Hoover, you admit that you used cocaine on the night of your arrest, don't you?

A: Yes, I admit it, but only because that rat, Reed, tricked me into it.

Q: But that wasn't the first time you used cocaine, was it?

Objection, your Honor. Cocaine use does not go to truth and veracity and as such cannot form the basis of specific act impeachment.

(Pause 3)

Vignette

43

Character—Fed. R. Evid. 412–413

David Jenkins has been charged with the sexual assault (rape) of Mary McKenna on June 4, 2003. Jenkins admits to having sexual intercourse with Ms. McKenna on that date, but claims that the act was consensual. During direct examination, Ms. McKenna testified that she and Jenkins were on a casual date and that when he took her home, he asked if could come into her apartment to use the bathroom. Once inside her apartment, McKenna further testified that Jenkins made a sexual advance towards her (hugging and attempting to kiss her and fondle her breasts) and she told him no several times and in no uncertain terms, and struggled to get out of his grasp. McKenna then stated that Jenkins carried her to her bedroom, threw her on the bed, and raped her. We pick up in the midst of the cross-examination of Ms. McKenna.

Q: You are eighteen years old, correct?

A: Yes.

Q: A freshman as Nita University?

A: Yes, that's right.

Q: You attended Lyman Hall High School in Nita?

A: Yes.

Q: You dated in high school beginning at age fourteen?

A: That's right.

Q: And you have been sexually active since the age of sixteen, correct?

(Pause 1)

Q: June 4, 2003 was not the first time you dated Mr. Jenkins, was it?

A: No, we dated in high school.

Q: You dated for most of your junior year, didn't you?

A: That's right.

Q: And for the period of December to June of that junior year you had consensual sexual relations with Mr. Jenkins, didn't you?

(Pause 2)

Q: You stated that during intercourse with Mr. Jenkins on June 4, 2003, he used a condom, correct?

A: Yes.

Q: And he was holding you down while he put on the condom?

A: I guess so, I couldn't move. I don't know what he was doing. I was trying to get away from him.

Q: You claim that he was rough with you?

A: Yes, he was. I was struggling.

Q: And as proof of that you say that you say that you had bruising in your vaginal area?

A: That's right.

Q: That bruising was noted the next day by a doctor who examined you during a previously scheduled appointment, right?

A: Yes.

Q: Now Ms. McKenna, you had a boyfriend in June 2003 other than Mr. Jenkins didn't you?

A: Your client wasn't my boyfriend. I had an exclusive relationship with Will Phillips at the time.

Q: And yet you went out to a bar with Mr. Jenkins?

A: As friends, nothing more and I told him so.

Q: You had a consensual sexual relationship with Mr. Phillips at the time?

(Pause 3)

Q: You had sex with Mr. Phillips on the afternoon of June 4, 2003, didn't you?

(Pause 4)

Q: You and Mr. Phillips have since broken up haven't you?

A: Yes we have.

Q: That was in late June 2003?

A: That's right.

Q: That's after Mr. Phillips contracted a sexually transmitted disease?

A: That's right.

Q: You had the same STD didn't you?

A: I guess I got it from Will?

Q: He claimed he got it from you, right?

A: He said that?

Q: You told him that you must have gotten the STD from Mr. Jenkins, correct?

A: I did say that?

Q: It was only after that quarrel with Mr. Phillips that you claimed that Mr. Jenkins raped you and went to the police, right?

A: I guess that was the timing.

Q: In fact, Ms. McKenna, you had many opportunities in the Spring of 2003 to contract an STD, didn't you?

A: Not at all, except from Will. We were exclusive beginning in January 2003.

Q: Isn't it a fact that you had sexual intercourse with at least four other men in the period between January and June of 2003?

(Pause 5)

A: That's a lie.

The cross-examination of Ms. McKenna concluded. The next witness for the government was Angela Jones. We pick up in the midst of Ms. Jones's direct examination by the prosecutor.

Q: Ms. Jones. Do you know a person by the name of David Jenkins?

.A: Yes I do. We dated in high school, in our sophomore year.

Q: That was three years ago?

A: That's right.

Q: How long did you date him?

A: Just a few months, three, I guess.

Q: Why did you stop dating him?

A: He was pressuring me to have sex with him and I didn't want to.

Q: Any other reason?

A: One night we were out at a school dance and we both had a little beer to drink in the car in the school parking lot, and we were making out, just kissing. He wanted to do more and grabbed at my breasts.

Q: What did you do?

A: I told him no and pushed him off.

Q: Then what happened?

A: He got mad and tore my blouse and started pulling at my jeans. I told him no again, but he just kept coming at me. I had no choice. I kicked him in the groin, and got out of the car and ran to the gym where the dance was going on and my friends helped me and got me home.

(Pause 6)

Q: After that did you tell anyone about what happened?

A: I warned my friends about him.

Q: Did you and your school friends talk about Mr. Jenkins and how he behaved with girls he was dating?

A: Yes.

Q: And among those friends of yours at the high school did Jenkins have a reputation regarding sexually assaultive behavior?

A: Yes, his reputation was for being very aggressive sexually, even when the girl he was with wasn't interested or told him to stop.

(Pause 7)

The government concluded its case and the defense called as its first witness, David Jenkins. Jenkins testified to his previous sexual relationship with Ms. McKenna and that on the evening of June 4, 2003, his sexual intercourse with Ms. McKenna was voluntary and consensual on her part. We pick up in the midst of Jenkins's direct examination.

Q: When was the last time you saw Ms. McKenna before June 4, 2003?

A: I would see her once in awhile. I go to Nita Community College but I go to social events, parties and the like at Nita U. And I would see Mary around campus.

Q: Do you know other people who know her?

A: Yes, lots of people. Everyone knows Mary.

Q: And during the period of January to June of 2003, did you speak with other people who knew Ms. McKenna?

A: Yes.

Q: And among those people did she have a reputation for sexual promiscuity?

(Pause 8)

Q: Based on talking with those people, did you believe that Ms. McKenna would have consensual sexual relations with you?

(Pause 9)

Q: Why did you believe that Ms. McKenna would have consensual sexual relations with you on June 4, 2003?

A: The way she was acting. She was willing and actively participating. I'd say she was the aggressor, not me although I was interested, I'll admit that. It was just like when we were in high school.

Q: How so?

A: We had sex at least seven times a week while we were dating. We couldn't keep our hands off of each other. She was willing to try anything at any time. Lots of times she started it.

(Pause 10)

Q: Any other reason?

A: Yes, I was told by at least three guys around that time that Mary was sexually active with them and other guys as well.

(Pause 11)

Vignette

44
Character—Fed. R. Evid. 415

John Jones and his employer, Flinders Aluminum Company, have been sued by Denise Dunston, a former employee of Flinders for gender discrimination. It is alleged that Mr. Jones created a hostile work environment for Ms. Dunston by continually making suggestive sexual remarks and touching her in a sexually offensive way. She further claims that on one occasion, after a business dinner, that the defendant attempted to rape her, tearing at her clothing and grabbing at her breast and genital area. Fortunately, she was able to fight him off and escape. The claim of hostile work environment against Flinders is predicated on the same facts.

Ms. Dunston has testified fully regarding the acts committed by Mr. Jones that created the hostile work environment. Included in Ms. Dunston's examination was testimony that on various occasions Mr. Jones touched Ms. Dunston's buttocks in an intentional way, on two occasions he intentionally brushed his hands across her breasts, and what she viewed as the attempted rape. The plaintiff was cross-examined, other evidence regarding her damages was presented, and the plaintiff has rested. Jones took the stand and testified essentially that none of the complained of activity occurred. We pick up in the midst of the cross-examination of Jones.

Q: Ms. Dunston is not the first woman employee you've harassed, is she?

A: I've never harassed anyone, Dunston included.

Q: Do you remember a woman by the name of Rachel Matthews?

A: I do, she used to work in my department. She left on her own; didn't like the job.

Q: In fact Sir, didn't you drive her out of the company?

A: Not a chance.

Q: Didn't you, on several occasions touch her shoulders in a sexually offensive way?

(Pause 1)

A: I may have touched her shoulder but it was not sexual.

Q: Didn't you accidentally brush up against her buttocks on several occasions?

(Pause 2)

A: Not that I can recall. If I did it was an accident.

Q: On the day before she resigned didn't you actually grab her buttocks and attempt to touch her genital area?

(Pause 3)

A: Not a chance.

The cross-examination continued with questions of Mr. Jones regarding numerous other occasions when he touched women employees in a sexually offensive way. On rebuttal the plaintiff calls Jennifer Patterson to the stand. We pick up in the midst of her direct examination.

Q: Do you know a person by the name of John Jones?

A: Yes, he's seated right over there.

Q: Let the record show that the witness has identified Jon Jones, the defendant. When did you meet Mr. Jones?

A: Five years ago at a bar in Nita City.

Q: What happened at that meeting?

A: We talked for awhile and had a few drinks. My girlfriends had to leave early and he offered me a ride home. I made it clear that I was only interested in a ride home.

Q: What happened when you arrived at your apartment?

A: I tried to get out of the car and he grabbed my arm, pulled me back in the car, and attempted to kiss me. I struggled and he grabbed at my clothes and tore my slacks and grabbed at my genital area.

(Pause 4)

Q: Were you able to get away?

A: Yes, I pushed him off, and ran into my apartment building.

Q: Did you complain to anyone about this encounter?

A: Yes to the owner/bartender at the bar where I met Jones.

Q: What did he say to you?

A: That he had banned Jones from the bar, that Jones had a reputation for being sexually aggressive towards women, and that several women had complained to him about Jones.

(Pause 5)

Vignette

45

Habit—Fed. R. Evid. 406

Plaintiff Mary Smith has sued the Nita Northern Railroad for the death of her husband, Marvin, at a train crossing owned by the railroad on Taylor Road, near the plaintiff's home. The collision occurred on a Saturday evening as the decedent drove home from a night baseball game of the Nita Nats. The crossing had warning lights but no automatic barrier. The lights were demolished in the collision between the train and the decedent's car and there is conflicting expert testimony about whether they were operating at the time of the collision. The train engineer, who survived the collision, has testified in a deposition that he saw the lights working and that the decedent was going pretty fast, didn't stop, and tried to beat the train. He further testified that the car stalled on the tracks making the collision unavoidable. Another witness who was about 50 yards from the crossing when the collision occurred, testified in a deposition that the lights were not working at the time of the collision. The plaintiff calls as her first witness, John Burnes. We pick up in the midst of Burnes's direct examination.

Q: Did you know Mary Smith's husband?

A: Of course. He was my neighbor, my friend, and we carpooled to work. Marvin drove in every morning. We worked in the same building downtown.

Q: Was Marvin a safe driver?

Objection.

(Pause 1)

Q: Do you know the railroad crossing where Marvin got killed?

A: I do, it's four blocks from our neighborhood. Marvin and I crossed those tracks at least twice a day. Once in the morning on the way to work and once on the way home.

Q: Was there any way that Marvin typically drove when he came to that railroad crossing?

A: There had been an accident at the crossing many years ago. Marvin always stopped at the crossing and looked both ways before crossing the tracks.

Motion to strike.

(Pause 2)

Q: Had you ever been in a car with Marvin in the evening on a weekend when he crossed those tracks?

A: Yes, maybe five or six times over the ten years I knew him.

Q: Did he drive any differently at that crossing on those occasions?

A: Not that I can remember.

Motion to strike.

(Pause 3)

Vignette

46

Offers to Compromise—Fed. R. Evid. 408

Plaintiff Harrison Sporting Goods, Inc. has sued Defendant Nita Sports, Ltd. in a contract action where Plaintiff claims that the Defendant company failed to deliver one hundred gross baseball bats at the price of $1,500 per gross in violation of their agreement to do so and as a result, Plaintiff had to secure replacement bats from another supplier at the price of $2,200 per gross. Defendant claims that there was no such agreement between the parties. The plaintiff put on its case and rested and the sales manager of Defendant company, Mary Gillespie, testified on direct examination that although there were conversations between her and representatives of the plaintiff company about purchasing bats there was no agreement reached. We pick up in the midst of plaintiff's cross-examination of Ms. Gillespie.

Q: You claim that there was no agreement between you and David Harrison regarding the purchase of bats?

A: That's right, we talked but never reached an agreement.

Q: Those conversations were in January 2003 about a delivery of bats for March of that year, correct?

A: Yes, that's right.

Q: The price discussed was $1,500 per gross for one hundred gross?

A: That's what he proposed but we never reached an agreement.

Q: In February 2003 you called Mr. Harrison and spoke with him?

A: Yes

Q: In that conversation, didn't you say to Mr. Harrison, 'I know we agreed on $1,500, but I can't deliver at that price, can you pay $2,000?'

Move to strike.

(Pause 1)

A: I never said any such thing.

Q: Mr. Harrison called you on March 1, 2003 inquiring about his shipment of bats?

A: Yes, and I told him we had no bats for him and there was no agreement.

Q: The two of you argued about whether there was an agreement?

A: Yes, briefly and then he hung up.

Q: You called Mr. Harrison the next day?

A: I did.

Q: You spoke about the disputed agreement?

A: We did.

Q: You told him that you regretted the misunderstanding and offered to give him a discount of 20 percent on his next shipment to, as you said, 'get his business back and avoid getting the lawyers involved.'

Motion to strike.

(Pause 2)

A: I wanted him to be our customer in the future, but we never had an agreement like he claimed.

Q: Your boss is quite upset about this dispute, isn't she?

A: Of course, no one like lawsuits.

Q: She's upset at you, correct?

A: That's fair.

Q: Your boss told you in March to get Harrison's business back?

A: She did.

Q: She said to offer him a small discount on a future order to try and appease him?

Objection. Motion to strike

Q: Your honor, we will connect this up in a few questions.

Judge: You may proceed. Answer the last question Ms. Gillespie.

A: She did say to offer a discount.

Q: When she heard about your March offer to Mr. Harrison of a discount of 20 percent on his next order to keep this disagreement out of the courts, she was angry with you because she thought 20 percent was too high and threatened to fire you if her company lost this case, didn't she?

Motion to strike.

(Pause 3)

Vignette

47

Offers to Compromise—Fed. R. Evid. 408

Franchisee has sued franchisor for fraud in the selling of a doughnut franchise. Franchisee claims that she was induced to purchase the franchise based in part on the franchisor's marketing materials which referred to construction of an upcoming highway which would in turn produce increased sales. The planned highway never materialized and plaintiff's profits have been meager. We pick up during the cross-examination of the plaintiff.

Q: Your contention is that you were induced to purchase the doughnut franchise based on statements made by the defendant, is that right?

A: Yes.

Q: You first discovered that the planned highway had been diverted to the other side of your community within a day of that decision having been made, didn't you?

A: Yes.

Q: You learned that fact from your cousin who is a member of the Nita State Legislature, didn't you?

A: Yes.

Q: And right away you wrote a letter to the defendant, didn't you?

A: Yes.

Q: (Handing the witness a copy of the letter): This document, Defendant's Exhibit A, is a copy of that letter, isn't it?

A: Yes.

Q: And in that letter, didn't you say . . .

(Assume that in the letter, plaintiff wrote the following: "I have friends in high places in Nita and I can make it extremely uncomfortable for your company to do business in Nita. I would be willing to forego alerting my contacts if you will return to me my purchase price plus 10 percent.")

Plaintiff's lawyer: Objection, your honor, plaintiff's statements in this letter are barred by Rule 408.

(Pause 1)

Q: Part of your claim for damages is that my client acted unreasonably in dealing with you, isn't it?

A: Yes.

Q: After you initiated this lawsuit, the defendant wrote you a letter, didn't it?

A: Yes.

Q: (Handing the witness Exhibit B), this is the letter my client sent you, isn't it?

A: Yes.

Q: Didn't my client say . . .

Plaintiff's Lawyer: Objection, this evidence is barred by Rule 408.

Assume that if allowed to finish the question, the defense lawyer would ask: In Exhibit B, doesn't my client offer to provide you a franchise at one of 3 alternate sites?

(Pause 2):

Vignette

48

Subsequent Remedial Measures—Fed. R. Evid. 407
Payment of Medical or Similar Expenses—Fed. R. Evid. 409
Liability Insurance—Fed. R. Evid. 411

Plaintiff Roger Albertson has sued the defendant, Angela Gould, for injuries he sustained when he fell down the stairs in his apartment complex. Plaintiff claims that his fall was caused by the defective condition of the stairway. Defendant claims that she was not the owner of the apartment complex, only its manager, and that she was not responsible for the maintenance of the stairway. She also claims that the plaintiff was responsible for his own injuries as there was nothing wrong with the stairway. The plaintiff has completed his case and rested. The defendant has testified that she was not the owner of the apartment complex, only its manager, and not responsible for stairway maintenance, and further that there was nothing wrong with the stairway in question. We pick up in the midst of the cross-examination of Ms. Gould.

Q: You were the person who found Mr. Albertson at the foot of the stairs?

A: I was. When he fell, he called out for help and I went to his aid.

Q: He was in considerable pain?

A: He appeared to be.

Q: You told him he should go to the hospital?

A: I offered to take him, but he said he couldn't afford it.

Q: You told him that the apartment complex would cover his medical expenses didn't you?

Objection.

(Pause 1)

Q: Mr. Albertson's glasses were broken in the fall, weren't they?

A: Yes, they were.

Q: You told Mr. Albertson that the apartment complex would pay to replace his glasses, didn't you?

Objection.

(Pause 2)

Q: Mr. Albertson's watch was broken in his fall, wasn't it?

A: Yes it was.

Q: You told Mr. Albertson that the apartment complex would pay to either repair or replace his watch; that there was insurance to cover the repair or replacement of the watch.

Objection.

(Pause 3)

Q: You have said there was nothing wrong with the stairs where Mr. Albertson fell, haven't you?

A: That's right.

Q: Didn't you have those stairs repaired by John Smith General Contractors three weeks after Mr. Albertson's fall?

Objection.

(Pause 4)

Q: You claim that the maintenance of the stairway was not your responsibility?

A: That's right.

Q: But didn't you repair those stairs yourself, five days after Mr. Albertson's fall?

Objection.

(Pause 5)

Q: You have claimed that you are not the owner of the apartment complex where Mr. Albertson fell, correct?

A: That's right.

Q: Didn't you have an insurance policy in your own name for liability coverage on that apartment complex in effect on the day that Mr. Albertson fell?

Objection. Motion for Mistrial.

(Pause 6)

Vignette

49

Liability Insurance—Fed. R. Evid. 411

Plaintiff David Kelly has sued the defendant, Grace Madison, for injuries he received in an automobile collision. Kelly testified that Madison's car ran a red light and side-swiped his car, and that as a result, Kelly suffered a serious whiplash injury. Kelly further testified that after the accident, Madison apologized to him, saying she was in a hurry to pick up her husband at the train station and ran the red light in her haste. We pick up in the midst of the direct examination of the plaintiff.

Q: What else did Ms. Madison say to you?

A: She told me that she was fully insured and that my car, and injuries I had, would be taken care of by her insurance.

Motion for mistrial.

(Pause 1)

Plaintiff then testified about his injuries and concluded his direct examination. We pick up in the midst of the cross-examination of the plaintiff.

Q: You spoke to an investigator after the accident, didn't you?

A: Yes.

Q: Didn't you give him a signed statement that the accident was unavoidable?

A: I signed a piece of paper that he wrote out after talking to me. I was in a hurry so I just signed it without reading it. I have seen the paper I signed and it does say that the accident was unavoidable but I never said that to him.

Defense counsel then had the plaintiff verify that Exhibit 7 was the statement he signed and introduced Exhibit 7 in evidence and ended the cross-examination. Plaintiff then presented the rest of his case and rested. The defense called as its first witness, Mike Walton, the investigator who took the plaintiff's statement referred to above, who testified that the plaintiff told him the accident was unavoidable and that the plaintiff carefully read the statement before signing it. We pick up during the cross-examination of Walton.

Q: Mr. Walton, you are not an independent investigator are you?

A: No.

Q: In fact you work for the Nita Casualty Insurance Company, don't you?

A: Yes, I do.

Q: And Ms. Madison has a $250,000 liability insurance policy with your company, doesn't she?

Motion for a Mistrial.

(Pause 2)

Vignette
50

Pleas and Plea Discussions—Fed. R. Evid. 410

Plaintiff James Corrigan has sued Defendant Roberta Jorgenson for injuries he received in an automobile collision. Plaintiff claims that the defendant was driving recklessly by driving at 55 miles-per-hour on a street where the speed limit was 35 miles-per-hour. Plaintiff also claims that the defendant was intoxicated at the time of the collision. Defendant denies speeding or driving while intoxicated and claims that the collision was caused by the plaintiff failing to yield the right of way to her. The plaintiff has completed presenting his evidence and has rested. The defendant has testified on direct examination and denied speeding or driving while intoxicated, and further, that the collision was caused by the plaintiff when he pulled out of a driveway in front of the defendant's car.

We pick up in the midst of the cross-examination of the defendant.

Q: You have testified today that you were charged by the police with speeding and DUI, but found not guilty by a jury, is that right?

A: Yes, that's right. I didn't do either of those things.

Q: You had a conversation with the prosecuting attorney the day of your trial, didn't you?

A: Yes

Q: You tried to persuade him to drop the charges against you?

A: I wasn't guilty.

Q: You told the prosecutor that you were speeding, but not drinking, correct?

Objection.

(Pause 1)

Q: You offered to plead nolo contendere to both charges if he would recommend that you keep your license, but when he refused to do so you withdrew your offer?

Objection.

(Pause 2)

Q: You did eventually plead guilty in your criminal case to speeding but when the judge refused to accept the prosecutor's recommendation on sentence, you withdrew that plea didn't you?

Objection.

(Pause 3)

Vignette
51

Attorney-Client Privilege—Fed. R. Evid. 501

Plaintiff Harriet Stevens has sued the defendant, Robert Wilson, for fraud. Plaintiff purchased a home from the defendant. Plaintiff claims that when asked directly about whether there was a problem with water in the basement of the home, the defendant assured her that it was a dry basement with no problems whatsoever. Plaintiff purchased the home and spent a considerable amount of money finishing the basement and installing very expensive electronic equipment. Several months after the work was completed, there were substantial rainstorms and the basement flooded, causing considerable damage. Defendant denies he had any knowledge of water problems in the basement. The case is now at trial and the plaintiff calls Defendant's former lawyer, Kate Patterson, as a witness. We pick up in the midst of the direct examination.

Q: Were you the defendant's original lawyer in this case?

A: Yes I was until I was discharged by him six months ago.

Q: Did you investigate the claim made by my client?

A: Yes, I did.

Q: Did you speak with the previous owner of the property in question?

A: Yes I did. It was very difficult to locate him, he had moved out of state without a forwarding address, but I did eventually find and talk to him.

Q: Did you ask him about whether there was ever any water in the basement of that property?

A: Yes I did.

Q: Do you know what happened to him?

A: Unfortunately he died in a car accident three months ago.

Q: What did the previous owner tell you about water in the basement?

Objection. Attorney-Client Privilege.

(Pause 1)

Q: After speaking with the previous owner did you talk to the defendant about what you had learned?

Objection. Attorney-Client Privilege.

(Pause 2)

A: Yes I did.

Q: What did the defendant tell you about what he had learned from the previous owner about water in the basement?

Objection. Attorney-Client Privilege.

(Pause 3)

Q: Was anyone else present when you talked to the defendant about your conversation with the previous owner?

A: Yes. His then fiancé. They are now married.

Q: What did the defendant tell you about what he had learned from the previous owner about water in the basement?

Objection. Attorney-Client Privilege.

(Pause 4)

Q: Did you receive interrogatories from me regarding this case?

A: I did.

Q: Was that before or after the previous owner of the property in question died?

A: Before he died and after I had talked to him.

Q: In response to those interrogatories did you provide his name and address to me?

A: I never had the opportunity to answer them. It was right after that time that I was discharged by the defendant.

Q: Did the defendant instruct you not to provide me with the address of the former owner before you were discharged?

Objection. Attorney-Client Privilege.

(Pause 5)

Q: Are you aware from any source other than your client of other allegations made against the defendant for fraud in the sale of real estate?

A: I did discover some information quite by accident at a social event right after I had been hired by the defendant.

Q: What was that information?

Objection. Attorney-Client Privilege

(Pause 6)

Vignette
52

Subsequent Remedial Measures—Fed. R. Evid. 407

Plaintiff Jack Price sues Defendant Shonda Motor Corporation for personal injuries arising from the defective design of the Shonda automobile in which Price was injured.

Price claims that the gas tank was defectively located too close to the rear-end of the automobile, making it subject to explosion upon a rear-end collision occurring at a speed of only 25 miles per hour. Plaintiff has called, adversely, the chief Shonda engineer who designed the model which is at issue in the lawsuit.

Q: Now Mr. Richards, as Shonda's chief design engineer on this project, did you make the final design decisions?

A: Yes.

Q: The issue of the placement of the gas tank was one of those decisions, wasn't it?

Objection, leading.

(Pause 1)

A: Yes.

Q: So it was you who determined that the gas tank would be placed toward the rear of the car?

A: Yes, but I had no choice, it was the only feasible and relatively safe place to locate it.

Q: And yet, only three years later, Shonda moved the gas tank in that model closer to the front end, didn't it?

Objection. That question calls for evidence of a subsequent remedial measure.

(Pause 2)

Vignette
53

Authentication—Fed. R. Evid. 901–902

Nine-year-old Jane Sanders and her parents bring an action against Charles Johnson for personal injuries. Jane was injured when she was hit by Johnson's automobile at 3 o'clock in the afternoon on September 1, 2003 as she was crossing the street near her elementary school. Jane claims she was crossing in the crosswalk with a green light at the intersection of Seventh and Green streets at the time of her injury. Plaintiffs call Rose Maguire, a school crossing guard, who was working at that intersection at the time of the accident.

Q: Please state your name.

A: Rose Maguire.

Q: What do you do for a living?

A: I have been a school crossing guard for the last five years.

Q: Are you familiar with the intersection at Seventh and Green streets?

A: Yes, I have worked that corner for the past three years.

Q: Were you at that intersection at approximately 3 P.M. on September 1, 2003?

A: Yes, I was.

Q: Showing you Plaintiff's Exhibit 1 for identification, tell us what it is.

A: It's a diagram of the intersection of Seventh and Green streets.

Q: *Your Honor, I offer Plaintiff's 1 as an exhibit.*

Objection.

(Pause 1)

Q: Ms. Maguire, showing what's been marked as Plaintiff's 2 for identification, please tell us what it is.

A: It's a photograph of the same intersection.

Q: I offer Plaintiff's 2 into evidence as an exhibit.

(Pause 2)

Vignette
54

Authentication—Fed. R. Evid. 901–902

We pick up in the midst of Plaintiff Parsons' testimony. Assume the same fact pattern as Vignette 2 (*Parsons v. Dornan*).

Q: Mr. Parsons, I show you a piece of paper that has been marked as Plaintiff's Exhibit 2. Do you recognize it?

A: Yes, it's a diagram of the intersection of Sixty-Eighth Street and Sherwood Avenue in the city.

Q: Did you make this diagram?

A: No.

Q: I offer this diagram in evidence as Plaintiff's Exhibit 2.

(Pause 1)

Vignette
55
Authentication—Fed. R. Evid. 901–902

Assume the same fact pattern as Vignette 2 (*Parsons v. Dornan*).

Q: Mr. Parsons, I show you this photograph previously marked as Plaintiff's 3 for identification. What is it?

A: It's a picture of the intersection of Sixty-Eighth Street and Sherwood Avenue.

Q: Who took this photograph?

A: I have no idea.

Q: Is it a fair and accurate representation of that intersection?

A: Yes.

Q: I move the admission of Plaintiff's 3 in evidence.

(Pause 1)

Objection. I'd like a voir dire examination concerning the photograph, Your Honor, prior to your ruling on its admission. I ask this be done outside the hearing of the jury.

(Pause 2)

Cross-examination of Parsons

Q: Mr. Parsons, showing you Plaintiff's 3 for identification, do you see any traffic lights in that photograph?

A: Why, no.

Q: Indeed, do you see a stop sign at the Sherwood Avenue entrances to the intersection?

A: Yes.

Judge, based on those questions, do you have any objection to the introduction of Exhibit 3 in evidence?

(Pause 3)

Q: On the date of the accident there were traffic lights at the intersection of Sixty-Eighth and Sherwood, weren't there.

A: Yes.

Q: Your honor, I object to the offer of Plaintiff's 3 as an exhibit.

(Pause 4)

Vignette
56

Authentication—Fed. R. Evid. 901–902, Firsthand knowledge—Fed. R. Evid. 602, Hearsay—Fed. R. Evid. 801, 803(6)

BMI, a giant corporation, is suing Minicom, a small company, for Minicom's failure to pay for three shipments of computer connector plugs, which BMI claims it sold to Minicom. Minicom defends, claiming that the first shipment was late, the second shipment was the wrong part, and the third shipment was never received. BMI calls Chris Kay, its Regional Sales Manager, who BMI alleges negotiated the Minicom contracts. We pick up in the midst of Kay's testimony.

Q: Now, Mr. Kay with respect to the first Minicom order which you have told us about, how did that sale come about?

A: Well, on January 12, 2003, Michael Lubell, the Vice President for purchasing of Minicom called me and placed an order for 3,500 BMI connector plugs at the price of $1.00 per plug.

(Pause 1)

Q: Mr. Kay, I show you an item previously marked as Plaintiff's Exhibit 1 for identification and I ask you what it is?

A: This is the page from my phone log dated January 12, 2003.

Q: Is there any entry on Plaintiff's Exhibit 1 for identification that refers to Minicom on that day?

A: Yes.

Q: What does the entry say?

(Pause 2)

Q: Mr. Kay, directing your attention to the second Minicom order you mentioned earlier in your testimony, how was that order initiated?

A: I received a letter from Mike Lubell on January 16, 2003.

Q: Showing you a document previously marked as Plaintiff's Exhibit 2 for identification, can you identify this document?

A: Yes, this is the letter from Lubell that I received at my office.

(Pause 3)

Q: Mr. Kay, after receiving Plaintiff's Exhibit 2 for identification what did you do?

A   I spoke with my assistant, Virginia Young, and she sent a letter to Lubell accepting the second order.

(Pause 4)

Q: Mr. Kay, showing you a copy of a document previously marked as Plaintiff's 3 for identification, can you identify it?

A: Yes, this is a copy of Ms. Young's letter to Lubell.

(Pause 5)

Q: Mr. Kay, directing your attention to the third BMI-Minicom transaction you mentioned in your earlier testimony, how did this transaction begin?

A: On January 20, 2003 I called Minicom and left a message with Lubell's secretary inviting Lubell to a golfing weekend at Hilton Head, South Carolina on February 8 and 9, 2003.

(Pause 6)

Q: Did you go to Hilton Head?

A: Yes.

Q: Who else was there?

A: A lot of our newer customers including Mr. Lubell and his wife.

Q: Did you have any conversation with Lubell?

A: Yes.

Q: Where?

A: In the clubhouse.

Q: Who else was there?

A: Just he and I.

Q: What did Lubell say to you?

A: He ordered 10,000 more interconnector plugs at $1 per plug for delivery within fourteen days.

(Pause 7)

Q: Did you say anything?

A: Yes, I accepted the offer on the usual terms.

After BMI rested, Minicom put in its case. Among other defenses, Minicom's Michael Lubell denied he had been at Hilton Head in February of last year and denied ever placing the order attributed to him in the clubhouse conversation. On rebuttal, BMI recalls Chris Kay to introduce a photograph of Kay and Lubell, which was allegedly taken at Hilton Head on February 8 or 9, 2003.

Your Honor, may the court reporter mark this as Plaintiff's 7 for identification and may I approach the witness?

Judge: *Yes.*

Q: Mr. Kay, I show you this photograph marked as Plaintiff's 7 for identification—can you identify it?

A: Yes, but I didn't take the photograph, the official Hilton Head photographer took it.

Q: What does Plaintiff's Exhibit 7 for identification show?

(Pause 8)

Vignette
57

Original Documents Rule—Fed. R. Evid. 1001–1006

The plaintiff, John Newman, was fired from his job as a state employment counselor. He filed a lawsuit against the state alleging that he was unlawfully discharged due to his unconventional religious beliefs in direct contravention of "The Governor's Guidelines for Employment Procedures." The state defends claiming that Newman was discharged because the state had cut its budget.

We join the trial now, while the plaintiff is on the witness stand testifying as to the events surrounding his discharge.

Q: Mr. Newman, are you familiar with the state's procedure for discharging its employees?

A: Yes, I am. All state employment practices are contained in "The Governor's Guidelines for Employment Procedures."

Q: How is it that you are familiar with the governor's guidelines?

A: Well, as a state employment counselor, I had to constantly refer to the Governor's Guidelines to inform people who sought advice.

Q: Are the guidelines for discharging employees mandatory or merely suggested procedures?

(Pause 1)

Q: Under the Governor's Guidelines are employee's personal beliefs allowed to be taken into account in discharge decisions?

(Pause 2)

A: No, the Guidelines specifically prohibit personal beliefs to be considered.

Q: Is there any reason to believe that in your case, your personal beliefs were considered?

A: Yes, the State Employment Commission sent a memorandum to Employment Counselors advising that State Employees would be fired if they actively believed in a cult religion.

Q: What exactly did this memorandum say?

(Pause 3)

Q: Turning to the administrative hearing on your discharge, are there written attendance records kept at these hearings?

A: Yes, there are.

Q: Do you remember who was there?

A: Yes.

Q: Who attended your hearing?

(Pause 4)

Vignette
58

Original Documents Rule—Fed. R. Evid. 1001–1006

Paul sues Daniels for breach of contract. Paul alleges Daniels failed to pay for floor tile sold under a written contract. We pick up in the midst of Paul's testimony.

Q: Mr. Paul, you have earlier testified that you and Daniels entered into a written agreement for the sale of the tile?

A: Yes.

Q: Do you have a copy of that agreement with you today?

A: No.

Q: Then, Mr. Paul, do you remember the terms of the agreement?

A: I do. I agreed to sell Daniels fourteen boxes of floor tile at $1,000 per box.

(Pause 1)

Q: Do you have the original of the contract?

A: No.

Q: Where is it?

A: My copy was destroyed in a fire at my plant.

Q: What did that contract provide?

(Pause 2)

Q: Who else had a copy of the contract?

A: Mr. Daniels did.

Q: What did the contract say?

Objection, we never received a subpoena for our copy of the contract and the plaintiff has the burden of proof.

(Pause 3)

After Paul rested, Daniels put on his case and called himself as a witness. We pick up in the midst of Daniels' testimony.

Q: Mr. Daniels, did you enter into any agreement with Mr. Paul to buy tiles?

A: Yes.

Q: Did you pay for the tiles?

A: Yes, $14,000 and I even got a receipt to prove it.

Objection—original document rule.

(Pause 4)

Vignette
59

Original Documents Rule—Fed. R. Evid. 1001–1006

John Harrison, the owner of an Army surplus store, has sued one of his suppliers, David Martin, for failing to deliver to Harrison 100 gross army blankets for which Harrison claims they had a contract. Martin admits that he made a written offer to sell the blankets, but contends that he did not receive Harrison's written acceptance within the time limit of the offer and therefore there was no contract. The plaintiff, Harrison, is on the stand and has testified that he received Defendant Martin's offer on September 1, 2003 to sell him the 100 gross blankets for $45,000. The offer letter provided that Harrison had to respond in writing before October 1, 2003. We pick up in the midst of the direct examination of Harrison.

Q: What did you do in response to Martin's offer?

A: I wrote a letter to him on September 20.

Q: Showing you what's been marked as Plaintiff's Exhibit 2 for identification, do you recognize it?

A: Yes, that's the carbon copy of the letter that I sent to Martin.

Q: What happened to the original?

A: It was mailed to Martin.

Q: Do you actually remember mailing the letter?

A: No.

Q: Did your business have a regular procedure for mailing letters in September 2003?

A: Yes. After the letter is typed I read it over for errors, check the address to make sure it is correct both on the letter and the envelope, sign it, and put the letter, the envelope, and the copy in my out box. My secretary then folds the letter, runs the envelope through our postage meter, and drops the letter in the postal slot outside our office. He then files the carbon in a file under the name of the addressee.

Q: When did you last see Plaintiff's Exhibit 2 for identification before you saw it in court today?

A: I took it out of our file on Martin before I came to court today.

Q: Your Honor, we made a request of the defendant to produce the original of Plaintiff's Exhibit 2 for identification and he has responded that he does not have it. We therefore offer Plaintiff's Exhibit 2 for identification into evidence.

(Pause 1)

Vignette
60

Summaries—Fed. R. Evid. 1006, Routine Business Practice—406

Plaintiff Eisler Engineering Company sues Defendant Amalgamated Engineering, a giant competitor, for antitrust violations, including violation of the Robinson-Patman Act, which forbids predatory price-cutting to eliminate competition. Amalgamated denies the allegations and at trial attempts to demonstrate that its pricing is not anti-competitive. Defendant Amalgamated calls its Chief Financial Officer, who has reviewed Amalgamated's sales records for the past ten years.

Q: What is your name?

A: Janet Perry.

Q: By whom are you employed?

A: I am employed by Amalgamated Engineering as its Chief Financial Officer—its chief accountant.

Q: Showing you what has been marked as Defendant's Exhibit 7 for identification, please tell the jury what it is.

A: This is a summary which I prepared of our sales records for the past ten years.

Q: How did you prepare this summary?

A: I looked at all of the records of our sales of our products which compete with Eisler for the past ten years, divided them by category and price, and tabulated all of this information in this summary.

Q: Your honor, I offer Defendant's Exhibit 7 in evidence.

Objection.

(Pause 1)

Q: After preparing Defendant's Exhibit 7, did you perform an analysis of your company's pricing structure during the ten-year period?

A: Yes, I did.

Q: What were you seeking to analyze?

A: I sought to determine the relative influence of a set of standard accounting variables on pricing decisions.

Q: After performing that analysis, did you come to an opinion about whether your company's pricing decisions were designed to be anti-competitive?

Objection.

(Pause 2)

Vignette
61
Hearsay—Fed. R. Evid. 801

The State has moved to involuntarily commit Richard Roe for mental health treatment. In support of its claim that Roe suffers from a mental disease or abnormality, the State has called Dr. Jane Bonner, a psychiatrist, to testify regarding her diagnosis. We pick up in the midst of Dr. Bonner's testimony.

Q: Dr. Bonner, have you interviewed Mr. Roe?

A: Yes, on two occasions.

Q: Please tell the court when these meetings took place.

A: Three weeks ago—June 21 and 22, 2004 at the State Treatment Center.

Q: Please tell us how the first meeting began.

A: I introduced myself as Dr. Bonner.

Q: Did Mr. Roe respond?

A: Yes, he said: 'I am the Emperor, Napoleon.'

Objection, hearsay.

(Pause 1)

Vignette
62

Hearsay—Fed. R. Evid. 801

Dennis McClain has sued Alexander Barber for personal injuries arising from an automobile collision. James Patterson is an eyewitness to the collision. The plaintiff has called Patterson as a witness. We pick up in the midst of Patterson's direct examination.

Q: Mr. Patterson, did you ever discuss the automobile collision with anyone before coming to court?

A: Yes. I discussed it with some people at work.

Q: When was that?

A: About three weeks after it happened.

Q: What did you say?

Objection. Hearsay.

Q: Your Honor, I am offering a statement from a witness who is present in court, subject to cross-examination. This isn't hearsay.

(Pause 1)

Vignette
63

Hearsay—Fed. R. Evid. 801, Limited Admissibility—Fed. R. Evid. 105

The government charges David Polk, a garment factory owner, with knowingly hiring an undocumented foreign national, Robert Alton. At trial, the government calls Charles Wall, one of Polk's employees, as a witness. We pick up in the midst of Wall's testimony.

Q: Mr. Wall, as an employee of David Polk, what are your duties?

A: I work a sewing machine and supervise other sewing machine operators.

Q: Directing your attention to the morning of July 2003, were you working that day?

A: Yes, I arrived at 8:30 A.M. as usual.

Q: When you arrived, what did you do?

A: I dropped by Mr. Polk's office and we talked. I told him that I had seen Bob Alton's immigration papers and that they were phony.

I object.

This is hearsay. The government can't prove Alton's an illegal alien with this out-of-court statement.

(Pause 1)

Vignette
64
Hearsay—Fed. R. Evid. 801

Mary Larson, the purchasing agent for a small radio manufacturer, Radiocom, Inc., called David Jones, Sales Manager for BMI, a large manufacturer of electronic parts, to place an order. Radiocom claims Larson placed an order and that BMI accepted it. When BMI failed to deliver, Radiocom sued for breach of contract. Radiocom calls Larson as a witness. We pick up in the midst of Larson's direct examination.

Q: Now Ms. Larson, do you know a person by the name of David Jones?

A: Yes, I do.

Q: Who is he?

A: He's the Sales Manager for BMI.

Q: When did you first meet him?

A: We met at a golf outing which BMI sponsored for prospective customers last September at a local country club.

Q: Did you speak with Jones at any time that day?

A: Yes, we spoke for about 45 minutes.

Q: Was anyone else present?

A: No.

Q: What did you say to Jones?

I object. Hearsay.

Q: (At sidebar) Your Honor, if permitted to answer, the witness will say that she ordered 100 gross transistors and that Jones agreed to deliver them for $100,000.

(Pause 1)

Vignette
65
Hearsay—Fed. R. Evid. 801

The government charges Senator Vincent Reston with bribery and claims that Senator Reston accepted a "bribe" from a government agent posing as a campaign contributor named George Carter. The senator defends on the basis that he knew the "contributor" was an agent and that he met with him to reject the offered bribe so as to enhance his reputation. Senator Reston claims he rejected the bribe while the government contends he accepted it. The agent was wired for the meeting, but the wire malfunctioned.

The defense calls an aide to the senator, Mary Richards.

Q: Ms. Richards, what do you do for a living?

A: I am an Administrative Assistant to Senator Reston.

Q: Were you working for the senator prior to August 14, 2002?

A: Yes.

Q: Do you recall any conversations with the senator about his meeting with a George Carter?

A: Yes, we discussed the meeting during the first week in August.

Q: What did the senator say?

Objection, hearsay.

A: He said: "I know this guy who calls himself 'Carter' is an FBI agent, but I'm going to meet with him so I can reject his money and get a clean bill of health from the government."

Q: Did you speak to the senator about the meeting with 'Carter' after the meeting on August 14?

A: Yes, he said this 'Carter' character really pressed him to accept the money, but he resisted the offer.

Move to strike the answer as hearsay.

Vignette
66

Hearsay—Fed. R. Evid. 801

On the night of April 1 Charles Wood drove his car off the road into a tree, killing one of his passengers, Clint Bronson. Bronson's estate brings a wrongful-death action against Wood alleging Wood's negligence. It has been stipulated that Wood was intoxicated at the time of the accident. His blood alcohol level was .18 percent. Wood defends on the basis that Bronson assumed the risk.

Burt Alcorn, a surviving passenger in Wood's car, was called by the plaintiff to explain the circumstances surrounding the accident. We pick up in the midst of Alcorn's cross-examination.

(Pause 1)

A: Yes.

Q: Didn't Wood respond that Bronson could get a cab if he was worried?

(Pause 2)

A: Yes.

Q: But Bronson still got in the car, right?

A: That's right.

Q: As you drove to the party, didn't Wood turn to Bronson and say, 'See, I told you I could drive?'

(Pause 3)

A: Yes, that's when we ran off the road.

Vignette
67

Hearsay—Fed. R. Evid. 801

The government is trying Marilyn Adams for the murder of Jim Jefferson. The case is circumstantial and a key in tying Adams to the killing is proof that the victim, Jefferson, was dead by 10 P.M. on August 1. Defendant calls Max Jefferson.

Q: Sir, what is your name and occupation?

A: Max Jefferson. I'm unemployed.

Q: Did you know the deceased victim, Jim Jefferson?

A: Yes, he was my brother.

Q: Directing your attention to the evening of August 1, where were you?

A: At home.

Q: Did you receive any phone calls that night?

A: Yes, one from my brother, Jim.

Q: What was the time of the phone call?

A: I don't remember.

Q: What did your brother say?

A: He said, 'This is a great episode of *Law and Order*, isn't it?'

Motion to strike as hearsay.

(Pause 1)

Q: I ask the court to take judicial notice of the fact that *Law and Order* is broadcast from 10–11 P.M. on Thursday evenings on Channel Three in Nita City.

Judge: *I take judicial notice of that fact.*

(Pause 2)

Vignette
68

Hearsay—Fed. R. Evid. 801

At the trial of Arnold Johnson for the murder of John Williams on Thanksgiving night at the victim's home at 2020 Main Street, the government calls Tom Smith as its first witness.

Q: What is your name and occupation?

A: Tom Smith, I'm a welder.

Q: Mr. Smith, do you know the defendant, Arnold Johnson?

A: Yes. We've known each other for years. We see each other about once a week.

Q: Did you see the defendant during the last week of November 2003?

A: Yes, I saw him on Thanksgiving day.

Q: Where did you see him?

A: We met at his house.

Q: Who was there?

A: Just Arnie, Tom Atkins, and I.

Q: Was there any conversation?

A: Atkins told Arnie he thought he knew who had beaten up Arnie's younger brother the day before and that it was John Williams.

(Pause 1)

Q: What did the defendant say?

(Pause 2)

A: He said he would 'get Williams.'

Q: Was there any other conversation?

(Pause 3)

A: The defendant asked me if I knew where he could find Williams, and I said he lives at 2020 Main Street.

(Pause 4)

Vignette
69

Hearsay—Fed. R. Evid. 801

Last year, Jack Rickels and Jim Watson attended a cocktail party hosted by Bob Snow. At the party, Rickels told Snow to keep an eye on his silverware because Watson was likely to steal it.

Watson learned of this conversation and brought suit against Rickels for slander. Watson has called the party host, Bob Snow, as a witness. We pick up in the midst of the direct examination of Snow.

Q: Mr. Snow, what did Rickels say to you?

A: He told me to keep an eye on my silverware because Watson was likely to steal it.

(Pause 1)

Q: What did you say?

A: I said, 'I hear you, but I can hardly believe it.'

(Pause 2)

Q: What happened then?

A: I told Rickels that I had to tell my wife what he just said to me and left the conversation and walked over to where she was standing.

(Pause 3)

Vignette
70

Hearsay: Consistent Statements, Offers of Compromise—Fed. R. Evid. 488, 801(d)(B)

Plaintiff Richard Parsons sues defendants Alf Bonds and Jack Chesney for assault and battery, claiming $100,000 in damages for very serious injuries. In his complaint, Parsons claims that Bonds and Chesney jointly assaulted and beat him outside of a bar in an unprovoked attack. Bonds and Chesney defend with self-defense and defense of another. Before trial, Chesney settled with Plaintiff, agreeing to pay a nominal amount in damages in exchange for a full release. At trial, the plaintiff calls Jack Chesney as a witness.

Q: Mr. Chesney, tell us how the fight began.

A: Well, Parsons had been saying some nasty things in the bar about the Orioles—Alf's favorite team. Alf was getting steamed and said he wouldn't mind taking a poke at Parsons if he got the chance.

Move to strike the answer as hearsay.

(Pause 1)

Q: What happened after that?

A: Alf and I went outside and hung around waiting for Parsons to leave the bar. When he did, Alf approached him and started pushing him around and then he really pounded on him.

Q: Did Parsons do anything to provoke the fight?

A: No, not really.

Q: Your witness.

Bonds' attorney then cross-examined Chesney.

Q: Now. Mr. Chesney, you haven't always said that Parsons was innocent in this fight, have you?

A: I don't know.

Q: In fact, didn't you say in your deposition, at page 18, lines 4 through 6, that 'Parsons came out of the bar looking for trouble, ran up to Bonds and started punching him'?

A: Yes, it says that.

Q: And just last week, after you gave your deposition, but before you testified in court here today, you, in fact, settled with Mr. Parsons didn't you?

Objection, this question calls for evidence of settlement or compromise negotiations.

(Pause 2)

A: Yes.

Q: And under the terms of the settlement, you agreed to pay Mr. Parsons $100, and he agreed to forget about trying to get $100,000 in damages from you for this beating, isn't that right?

A: Well, yes.

Plaintiff's counsel then examined Mr. Chesney on Re-direct.

Q: Mr. Chesney, did you speak to a police officer immediately after the incident in this case?

A: Yes.

Q: What did you tell the officer?

A: That Bonds started the fight.

(Pause 3)

Vignette
71

Hearsay: Statements of Identification—Fed. R. Evid. 801(d)(1)(C)

The government has charged Robert James with armed robbery of an armored car. James' defense is alibi, and thus, the identity of the robber is a key issue. At trial, the government calls David Ross, an eyewitness.

Q: Mr. Ross, did you speak to the police at the scene of the robbery?

A: Yes, about 10 minutes after it occurred.

Q: Did you give them a description of the robber?

A: Yes.

Q: What did you tell the police?

Objection, hearsay.

(Pause 1)

A: I told them he was a white male, 6 feet tall or 6 feet and 1 inches tall. He had black hair and a scar on his right cheek.

Q: At the time you gave the description, was there a police artist present who was making a drawing?

A: Yes, she drew as I talked.

Q: Did you look at the drawing when she finished?

A: Yes, and I made a few corrections.

Q: Showing you what's been marked as Government's 1 for identification, is this the drawing you just described?

A: Yes, it is.

Q: What did you say when the artist first showed you the drawing?

Objection.

(Pause 2)

Vignette
72

Hearsay: Admissions—Fed. R. Evid. 801(d)(2)

The Capper Beer Corporation and its President, Bob Capper, are on trial for alleged antitrust violations. The prosecution contends that Roberta Capper engaged in price fixing negotiations with Jack Rollins, President of the Rollins Beer Corporation. Neither Mr. Rollins nor his company has been indicted.

In its case in chief against Roberta Capper, the prosecution has called Capper's former secretary, Ronald Janko, to testify as to the events surrounding the price fixing negotiations. We pick up in the midst of Janko's testimony.

Q: Mr. Janko, describe your duties when you worked as Ms. Capper's secretary.

A: I answered her phone and typed her correspondence. I also placed outgoing calls for her.

Q: Mr. Janko, showing you what has been marked as Government's Exhibit 1 for identification, can you identify it?

A: Yes, this is a letter I typed for Ms. Capper last May.

Q: Do you recognize the signature?

A: Yes, it's Ms. Capper's.

Q: Your Honor, I offer this letter as Government's Exhibit 1.

Your Honor, we object to this letter as hearsay and may we approach the bench?

Judge: *You may. Let's see—the letter is from Roberta Capper to Jack Rollins of the Rollins Beer Corporation. It says: 'Dear Jack: We intend to hold the price of our six pack to $3.75 for the next twelve months. What's your position? Sincerely, Roberta Capper.'*

(Pause 1)

Q: Mr. Janko, while you were typing this letter, were you alone?

A: No, Jim Jackson, our national sales manager, was waiting to see Ms. Capper and he was looking over my shoulder as I typed the letter.

Q: Did he say anything to you?

A: Yes.

Q: What?

A: He said, I'm glad that Capper finally has acted on my negotiations with Rollins.

(Pause 2)

Q: Mr. Janko, do you know Jack Bush?

A: Yes, he's the former Vice-President of our company.

Q: When did you last see him?

A: About three days after I typed this letter here.

Q: When you say 'this letter' do you mean Government's Exhibit 1?

A: Yes.

Q: What were the circumstances of your meeting Mr. Bush that day?

A: The day after I sent the letter to Rollins Beer, Bush came in to see Ms. Capper.

Q: Did they have a conversation?

A: Yes, right in my office.

Q: What did Mr. Bush say?

A: Mr. Bush had heard about the price fixing and he was real mad. He accused Capper of breaking the law by fixing prices.

(Pause 3)

Q: What did Capper do?

A: Ms. Capper didn't say anything. She just nodded his head up and down and smiled.

(Pause 4)

Q: Did you discuss this letter with Ms. Capper?

A: Yes, after I was approached by the FBI I told him the feds were looking into Capper's pricing.

(Pause 5)

Q: How did Ms. Capper react when he found out that there was a federal investigation of Capper Beer and price fixing?

A: She panicked.

Q: Could you explain?

A: Well, when she found out about the investigation she asked me to gather up the Rollins correspondence files. Then we both went down to the paper shredder and we spent the afternoon shredding documents.

(Pause 6)

Q: Mr. Janko, do you know if Mr. Rollins of Rollins Beer ever received Ms. Capper's letter?

A: Yes, he got it.

Q: How do you know that?

A: Well, I called him and asked him if he had received it. I know his voice from talking to him many times before on the phone and in person. He said he had gotten it.

Q: Did he say anything else?

A: Yes. He said that he would like to make a few changes in the agreement, but that $3.75 was a good price to set for the product.

(Pause 7)

Q: Was there any other conversation?

A: Yes, Mr. Rollins said that he intended to meet with Ms. Capper the next day to finalize the agreement.

Q: Anything else?

A: Yes. Rollins said that he had been very happy with the previous agreements with Ms. Capper and hoped this one would work out as well.

(Pause 8)

Vignette
73

Hearsay: Party Admissions—Fed. R. Evid. 801(d)(2)

"Big Tuna" Parcells is on trial for drug possession based on his arrest in the home of "Big Dog" Johnson, where a large stash of drugs was found by police. At trial, Big Tuna's lawyer asks the following questions of a police officer involved in the investigation and arrest.

Q: Now Sergeant Natali, you are the officer who submitted the affidavit I support of the search warrant in this case, didn't you?

A: Yes.

Q: And in that affidavit in support of a search warrant, you stated that the premises to be searched belonged to Anthony "Big Dog" Johnson didn't you?

A: Yes.

Q: And that affidavit included the report from a confidential informant?

A: Yes.

Q: And your affidavit stated that the informant told you that the person who owned and possessed the drugs was Anthony Johnson, isn't that right?

Objection, hearsay within hearsay.

(Pause 1)

Vignette
74

Hearsay: Admissions—Fed. R. Evid. 801(d)(2)

Boyer Pharmaceuticals and its President, Arthur Boyer, have been sued by a competitor, Charles Aspirin Co. for a civil antitrust violation. Charles claims that the defendants agreed to set prices with another competitor, Painfree, Inc., for their aspirin substitutes. Painfree is not a party to the lawsuit, having settled with Charles before filing of the suit against Boyer and Boyer Pharmaceuticals.

At trial, Charles calls Mary Rogers, the CEO of Painfree.

Q: Ms. Rogers, are you familiar with a man named Arthur Boyer?

A: Yes, I know him as the President of Boyer Pharmaceuticals.

Q: Have you spoken to him in the past ?

A: Yes, I have spoken to him both in person and on the telephone.

Q: Do you recall speaking to Mr. Boyer on the telephone on April 1, 2001.

A: Yes, I do.

Q: What did he say to you?

A: He asked if I was interested in 'making a little money together?"

(Opponent):   *Your Honor, I ask you to instruct the jury to consider this statement only against Mr. Boyer personally and not as against the corporate defendant.*

(Pause 1)

Q: Did he say anything else?

A: Yes, he asked if we were planning any price increases in the next year.

Q: What did you say?

Objection. Hearsay.

(Pause 2)

A: I said that we were going to raise prices in about two months. He said that maybe we should coordinate that effort.

Q: Did you ever have any conversations with any other representatives of Boyer Pharmaceuticals?

A: Yes, I spoke to Mary Richards, their Vice President for Marketing about a week after the conversation with Boyer.

Q: What did she say?

Objection. Hearsay.

(Pause 3)

A: She said that she was following up on Boyer's conversation with me and that Boyer planned on raising its wholesale price by 15 percent in about two months.

Vignette
75

Hearsay: Admissions—Fed. R. Evid. 801(d)(2)

Plaintiff James Earl brings a civil rights action against three police officers and their employer-municipality. Earl claims that the officers systematically harassed and threatened him by conducting illegal arrests and searches to intimidate Earl into discontinuing a relationship with a sister of one of the officers. The officers are Robert Avery, James Barrett, and Ray Chester. A fourth officer, Henry Davis, resigned from the police force and settled with the plaintiff before trial. Plaintiff calls Davis as a witness.

Q: Now, Mr. Davis, during the last three years of your service as a police officer, did you have a regular partner?

A: Yes. Robert Avery.

Q: Did you know the other defendants, James Barrett and Ray Chester?

A: Yes, we usually worked the same shift over the last few years.

Q: Did you ever have any conversations with Avery about the plaintiff, James Earl?

A: Yes.

Q: Please state the substance of those conversations.

Objections, hearsay.

(Pause 1)

A: Avery asked if I wanted to go out one night while we were on patrol and roust James Earl. I asked why and he said it was 'personal.' I told him I would do it if it was important to him, and he said it was.

Move to strike the witness's reporting his own statements as hearsay.

(Pause 2)

Q: Did you act on the conversation?

A: Yes, Avery and I went out to the plaintiff's trailer, where we were met by officers Barrett and Chester, and we proceeded to toss the interior of the plaintiff's trailer.

Q: By 'toss' what do you mean?

A: Search it and toss everything upside down.

Q: Did you have any law enforcement reason to conduct this search?

A: No, we did not.

Q: Did anybody say anything?

A: As we left, Barrett said to the plaintiff, 'This will teach you to mess with Avery's little sister.'

(*Avery and Barrett's counsel*):   *Move to strike the statement as inadmissible hearsay as to my client.*

(Pause 3)

(*Municipality's counsel*):   *Move to strike as inadmissible hearsay as to the Municipality.*

(Pause 4)

Vignette
76

Hearsay: Admissions—Fed. R. Evid. 801(d)(2)(E)

James Mitchell and two codefendants, Martin Jones and Charles "Lefty" Smith, are on trial for armed robbery of a bank. For purposes of this vignette, assume that you are the defense counsel for Mitchell only. The government calls a city police officer as a witness.

Q: What is your name and occupation?

A: Bobby Crocker, detective with the city police department.

Q: Directing your attention to the morning of April 18, 2003, where were you that morning?

A: In response to a radio call that said there was a robbery in progress, I went to the Second National Bank at Fifth Avenue and Forty-Second Street.

(Pause 1)

Q: When you got there, what did you see?

A: I saw three men leave the bank and jump into a waiting car.

Q: Are those men in the courtroom today?

A: Yes, right over there.

Q: Let the record show that the witness has identified the defendants as James Mitchell, Martin Jones, and Charles Smith.

Q: What did you do after the defendants got into the car?

A: I pursued them in my car for a few blocks until it ran into an embankment and stopped.

Q: What happened next?

A: Lefty Smith jumped out and yelled to the others, 'Scatter, I'll take the money.'

(Pause 2)

Q: Was there any other conversation?

A: Yes, as Marty Jones jumped out of the car, he yelled to Mitchell: 'Damn it, Jim, when you got us together to plan this job, you said it was foolproof.'

(Pause 3)

Q: Then what happened?

A: I ran after Lefty Smith, the guy who took the money, and I caught him. Before I could even give him the Miranda warnings, he said: 'I didn't want to rob the bank, but the other guys made me.'

(Pause 4)

Vignette
77

Hearsay: Admissions—Fed. R. Evid. 801(d)(2)(B)

The defendant, Bob Bram, is on trial for the murder of Bill Darwin. At trial, the government calls the arresting officer.

Q: What is your name and occupation?

A: I am James Kelly. I am a city police detective-sergeant attached to homicide.

Q: Were you on duty on the evening of April 20 at about 10 P.M.?

A: Yes.

Q: What were you doing at that time?

A: I arrested the defendant here, Bob Bram, outside a bar on Halstead Street and gave him his *Miranda* warnings.

Q: Was anyone else present?

A: Yes, a woman named Nancy Moore.

Q: Did Nancy Moore say anything to you in the presence of the defendant?

(Pause 1)

A: Yes, she said she had seen the defendant having an argument with Bill Darwin, the victim, inside the bar fifteen minutes before the shooting.

Vignette
78

Hearsay: Present Sense Impression—Fed. R. Evid. 803(1)

Jane Jackson sues John Drake for trespassing. The plaintiff has called Jane's brother, Bob Jackson, as its first witness.

Q: What is your name and address?

A: Bob Jackson, 10 Main Street.

Q: Directing your attention to the evening of July 18, 2003, where were you?

A: At home.

Q: Did you receive any telephone calls?

A: Yes, one.

Q: Who was it?

A: My sister, Jane.

Q: What did she say?

A: She told me she could see a man lurking in the garden outside her window. She said he'd been there for a couple of minutes.

(Pause 1)

Q: What did you say?

(Pause 2)

A: I asked who it was. She said, 'It looks like John Drake.' Then she hung up.

(Pause 3)

Q: What did you do?

A: I called back about fifteen minutes later and got her back on the line and I asked her 'What happened?'

Q: What did she say?

A: She said she had gone outside right after our earlier phone call and had seen tracks of a man's shoes in the garden.

(Pause 4)

Q: Did she say anything else?

A: Yes, she said she heard a voice she recognized as Drake's nearby saying, 'Let's beat it.'

(Pause 5)

Vignette
79

Hearsay: Present Sense Impressions—Fed. R. Evid. 803(1)

Plaintiff Bob Jackson has sued Defendant Robert Potter for personal injuries arising from an automobile collision. Plaintiff is claiming lost wages as part of his damages, asserting that he can no longer perform his job as an airline mechanic because of his injuries. Defendant believes Jackson is malingering and at trial calls its investigator as a witness.

Q: Tell us your name, Sir.

A: James Rockfish. I am a private investigator.

Q: Are you familiar with the plaintiff in this case, Bob Jackson?

A: Yes, I was asked to watch Mr. Jackson and talk to his neighbors to see if he was able to perform physical work despite his alleged injuries.

Q: How did you perform your investigation?

A: I surveilled Mr. Jackson's home and made contact with his neighbors. I asked his immediate neighbors to call me if they saw him performing any physical labor around the house.

Q: Did any neighbor ever call you?

A: Yes, a Ms. Alice Smith called me on Saturday morning, April 5, 2004, to report on Mr. Jackson

Q: What did Ms. Smith tell you?

Objection, hearsay and lack of foundation.

(Pause 1)

Q: How did you know it was Ms. Smith calling?

A: I have caller identification on my phone and she also identified herself. She said: "I'm looking out my window and I can see my neighbor Mr. Jackson up on a ladder cleaning his gutters."

Objection, move to strike the answer as hearsay.

(Pause 2)

Q: Did she say anything else?

A: Yes, she said that she had seen him doing the same thing the week before.

Move to strike the answer as hearsay.

(Pause 3)

Q: Did you ever speak to Ms. Smith again?

A: Yes, she called the next day to tell me that she had asked Mr. Jackson if he would clean her gutters if she paid him and he said he was feeling much better and he would be glad to do the work.

Move to strike the answer as hearsay.

(Pause 4)

Vignette
80

Hearsay: Excited Utterances—Fed. R. Evid. 803(2)

Paul Prince sues Doris Drake for personal injuries for property damage and Prince's personal injuries arising from an automobile collision. At trial, Prince calls an eyewitness to testify.

Q: What is your name, sir?

A: David Walton. I live at 533 Winding Lane in the city.

Q: Where were you at 2 P.M. on the afternoon of August 23, 2003?

A: I was waiting for the light to change at the intersection of First Avenue and Pine Street here in town.

Q: Did anything unusual happen while you waited for the light?

A: Yes, there was an automobile collision. It involved the plaintiff's and defendant's automobiles.

Q: What did you do after you saw the collision?

A: I ran into the intersection to see if anyone was hurt.

Q: What happened next?

A: When I got to the plaintiff's car, he looked at me from the driver's seat with blood streaming down his face, and said, 'My God, she just ran that red light.'

Move to strike the last sentence as hearsay.

(Pause 1)

Q: What happened next?

A: The ambulance arrived and after the EMS personnel administered first aid, they prepared to take the plaintiff to the hospital. As the ambulance pulled away, about twenty minutes after the collision, the plaintiff shouted: 'I can't believe the carelessness of that other driver.'

Move to strike the answer as hearsay.

(Pause 2)

Vignette
81

Hearsay: Excited Utterances—Fed. R. Evid. 803(2)

Janet Thacker sues Mary Perone and John Stiller for assault and battery. Ms. Thacker was found unconscious with severe head injuries after having been brutally beaten. She immediately underwent a complex brain operation and was in a coma for seven days. When she finally regained consciousness, Ms. Thacker spoke with her brother Steven about the attack.

The plaintiff has called Steven Thacker to relate his conversation with his sister. We pick up in the midst of the direct examination of Mr. Thacker.

Q: Mr. Thacker, what happened on the seventh day after Janet's operation?

A: Well, she came out of her coma while I was sitting there and was able to speak.

Q: Who was in the room with her when she awoke?

A: Just me. It was late at night and everyone else had gone home.

Q: Did you call a doctor?

A: Not immediately. I wanted to talk to her first.

Q: What happened when she woke up?

A: She said 'Please stop hitting me Mary, what did I ever do to you?'

(Pause 1)

Q: Then what happened?

A: Well, I walked over to her and showed her a picture of the defendant, John Stiller, that the police had left in the room. They told me that they thought Stiller was one of Janet's attackers.

(Pause 2)

Q: What happened?

A: The second she saw the picture she began to scream and cry. She kept on saying, 'It's him! He tried to kill me!'

(Pause 3)

Vignette
82

Hearsay: State of Mind, State of Mind for Diagnosis—Fed. R. Evid. 803(3)–803(4))

Vincent Baker sues the Veterans' Administration and Frances Knight, a former nurse at a V.A. Hospital. Mr. Baker alleges that he suffered physical harm because Ms. Knight poisoned Baker's food when he was a patient in the VA Hospital.

The plaintiff calls his treating physician who first discovered the poison. We pick up in the midst of the doctor's testimony.

Q: Did you see the victim on April 1, 2003?

A: Yes.

Q: When did you first see him?

A: He was the first person I saw on my nightly rounds. I saw him at 6:30—right after dinner.

Q: What happened when you saw him?

A: I asked him how he was feeling. He said he was feeling bad. So, I checked his pulse and saw that it was extraordinarily slow.

(Pause 1)

Q: Then what happened?

A: Well, I became concerned. I asked him when he began to feel badly. He said he began to feel bad right after dinner.

(Pause 2)

Q: What did you do then?

A: Well, I looked at the remaining food on his dinner tray. The food had a small amount of a white, powdery substance on it. I thought it was poison.

Q: What happened then?

A: I asked him who had brought him his dinner tray.

Q: What did the patient say?

(Pause 3)

A: He said that Frances Knight had brought in his dinner tray.

Vignette
83

Hearsay: Exceptions—Fed. R. Evid. 803(2)–(4)

David Plante, the plaintiff, sues Barbara Davis, the defendant, for personal injuries suffered when Davis' automobile struck Plante, a pedestrian. At trial, Plante offers himself as a witness. We pick up in the midst of his testimony.

Q: Mr. Plante, what happened immediately after you were struck by the Davis automobile?

A: I sat up, a little dazed, and said: 'My God, she was going way too fast.'

Move to strike as hearsay.

(Pause 1)

Q: Then what happened?

A: Davis jumped out of her car, rushed up to me and asked if I was all right. I said, 'My leg is killing me.'

Move to strike as hearsay.

(Pause 2)

Q: What happened next?

A: A police officer arrived about 5 or 6 minutes later and asked my how I was doing. I said I was calming down, but that I might be going into shock.

Move to strike as hearsay.

(Pause 3)

Q: Did you ever get medical help?

A: Yes, the paramedics arrived.

Q: Did you speak to them?

A: Yes.

Q: What did you say to the paramedics?

Objection, hearsay.

(Pause 4)

A: I told them my leg was killing me, my head ached, and I was feeling dizzy. I then passed out and woke up in the hospital. I said that if the other driver hadn't been out of control, I might have had a chance.

Move to strike the last sentence of the answer.

(Pause 5)

Q: How long were you in the hospital?

A: About three weeks.

            ***

Q: After leaving the hospital, did you ever see any other doctors?

A: I only saw the doctor my lawyer asked me to see.

Q: Did she take a history?

A: Yes, she asked me to describe by condition and health before the accident?

Q: What did you tell her?

Objection, hearsay.

(Pause 6)

Vignette
84

Hearsay: Recorded Recollections—Fed. R. Evid. 803(5)

This is a trial in a tort action for negligence brought by David Smith against the Jones Moving Company. Smith claims that the movers damaged a number of items of personal property in moving Smith's household goods. Jones Moving Company's attorney has called Nick Strong, one of the Jones Moving Company's employees who actually performed the move.

Q: What is your name and occupation?

A: Nick Strong. I'm a truck driver and laborer for the Jones Moving Company.

Q: Directing your attention to September 1, 2003, did you have any jobs that day?

A: Yes, we moved Mr. Smith's stuff.

Q: Were any of Mr. Smith's items damaged?

A: Yes, I believe a few were.

Q: Do you remember what those items were?

A: No way, I've done a hundred jobs since then.

Q: Mr. Strong, I show you this document, previously marked as Defendant's Exhibit 3 for identification. Can you identify it?

A: Yes, it's a list of Smith's items damaged in the move.

Q: Did you make the list?

A: No.

Q: Who did?

A: John Weak who was working with me that day. I watched him write it.

Q: Did you inspect the items on the list after Mr. Weak wrote it up?

A: Yes.

Q: When was the list made?

A: About an hour and a half after we left Smith's house and got back to our warehouse.

Q: Do you know today whether the list was accurate when it was made?

A: I can't actually remember, but I take these lists very seriously whenever I make them because they are often the subjects of lawsuits.

Q: Your honor, I offer this list into evidence as Defendant's Exhibit 3 for identification into evidence.

(Pause 1)

Q: Were there any additional items of Smith's damaged?

A: Yes, I think so.

Q: Can you remember what they were?

A: No way.

Q: Now I show you this document previously marked as Defendant's Exhibit 4. Can you identify it?

A: Yeah, this is a supplementary list of Smith's damaged items.

Q: Who made it and when?

A: Weak made this a day after the move. I recognize his handwriting. I went to Smith's house by myself and looked at the items. I then called Weak on the phone at the office and told him about the twelve additional damaged items and I told him to write down these items on the list.

Q: Your Honor, I offer Defendant's Exhibit 4 for identification in evidence.

(Pause 2)

The defendant-mover now calls John Weak. We pick up in the midst of Weak's testimony.

Q: Mr. Weak, were you working on the day after David Smith's move?

A: Yes.

Q: Where?

A: I was in the office all day.

Q: Did you receive any phone calls that day?

A: Yes.

Q: Do you remember the names of any one of those callers?

A: Well, I remember that Nick Strong called in saying he was calling from Smith's new house and named about a dozen damaged items.

Q: What did you do when Nick named the items?

A: When he named each one, I wrote it down on a list.

Q: Then what action did you take?

A: I read each item back to Nick right after putting it on the list to make sure I had it right.

Q: Mr. Weak, do you know today that the list was accurate when it was made?

A: Yes—I always take great care in keeping track of customer damage complaints.

Q: Mr. Weak, showing you a document previously marked as Defendant's Exhibit 4 for identification, can you identify it?

A: Yes, this is the list I just described of Smith's damaged furniture—the list I took over the phone from Nick Strong.

Q: Your Honor, I offer Defendant's Exhibit 4 for identification in evidence.

(Pause 3)

Vignette
85

Hearsay: Business Records—Fed. R. Evid. 803(6))

Jon Baker, the Executive Director of REPAC, a local antipoverty agency, has been indicted on charges of illegally diverting federal funds from the agency to his own use. At Baker's trial, the government seeks to offer records kept by the agency of its receipts and expenditures. The government calls Robert Richardson, an accountant, as its first witness.

Q: What is your name and occupation?

A: Robert Richardson, I am a certified public accountant.

Q: Mr. Richardson, are you familiar with an agency called REPAC?

A: Yes, I had a contract to do their books and oversee its non-profit status for the past two years.

Q: Mr. Richardson, I show you this ledger book that's been marked as Government's Exhibit 1 for identification and ask you if you can identify it?

A: Yes, it is REPAC's financial ledger for the past two years.

Q: Mr. Richardson, do you know how Government's Exhibit 1 for identification is made and kept?

A: Yes, the ledger is kept in my office and I make entries in those books whenever I receive a call from either the defendant, Mr. Baker, or his deputy director. If they tell me that funds were received, I make the relevant entry with amount and date. If they tell me money was disbursed, I make the appropriate entry. I did this for the last two years.

Q: Your Honor, I offer Government's Exhibit 1 for identification as Government's Exhibit 1.

(Pause 1)

Vignette
86

Hearsay: Records of Regularly Conducted Activity—Fed. R. Evid. 803(6)

Plaintiff Susan Pender sues Defendant Dynamic Electronics (Dynamic) for racial discrimination. Pender claims she did not receive a promotion for which she was qualified because of her race. She is African-American.

After Plaintiff has put on her direct case, Defendant calls Janet Jankowski, Director of Personnel for Dynamic. We pick up in the midst of Ms. Jankowski's direct examination testimony.

Q: Ms. Jankowski, I show you Defendant's Exhibit 3 for identification, and I show a copy to Defense Counsel. Ms. Jankowski, please tell us what Defendant's 3 is.

A: It's a response which we filed to the EEOC complaint filed by Ms. Pender. The response is contained in a form provided by the EEOC.

Q: Who filled out that form?

A: My assistant, John Thomas.

Q: Has your office filed such forms before?

A: Yes, I would say we have filed three or four over the past ten years.

Q: Who ordinarily completes the form?

A: The Personnel Director or her assistant.

Q: Where do you get the facts which make their way into the EEOC form?

A: Either from my personal knowledge or from discussions with the employee's supervisor.

Q: What is done with the forms after your office completes them?

A: We save a copy for the personnel file, we send the original to the EEOC, and we send a copy to our legal counsel.

Q: Your honor, I offer Defendant's 3 as an exhibit.

Opposing Counsel: Objection, hearsay and I would like a short voir dire.

(Pause 1)

Court: Proceed.

Opposing Counsel: Ms. Jankowski, you send a copy to legal counsel because you ordinarily anticipate litigation when an employee files an EEOC complaint, don't you?

A: Well, yes.

Opposing Counsel: I object. This document is hearsay.

(Pause 2)

Vignette
87

Hearsay: Records of Regularly Conducted Activity—Fed. R. Evid. 803(6)

Peters has brought an action for personal injuries and property damage to his automobile against National Foods Corporation resulting from an accident in which a National Foods truck rear-ended Peters' automobile.

At the trial, Davis, the defendant, calls John Jones, an employee of National Foods.

Q: Please tell us your name and occupation.

A: I am John Jones and I am employed by National Foods. I'm in charge of investigating claims, including those growing out of auto accidents that are made against National or its employees while on the job.

Q: When an automobile accident involving National is reported to you, what do you do?

A: I go out and investigate the damage and cause of the accident and then write up and file a report that is maintained in the company's permanent files.

Q: How many of these reports have been filed in the last twelve months

A: About seventy-five.

Q: Who did the report on the accident involved in this case?

A: I did.

Q: I show you a document marked as Defendant's Exhibit 1 for identification and ask you if you recognize it?

A: Yes, this is the report of the accident in this case.

Q: Your Honor, I offer Defendant's Exhibit 1 for identification as Defendant's Exhibit 1.

(Pause 1)

Vignette
88

**Hearsay: Official Records, Statements Made Under Belief of Impending Death,
Hearsay within Hearsay—
Fed. R. Evid. 803(8), 804(b)(2), 805**

The defendant, Jackie Carney, has been sued civilly for wrongful death and conversion for activities involving an armed bank robbery and felony murder. Carney was found not guilty of all criminal charges. The plaintiff has called Police Desk Captain Frank Cannon who is in charge of all desk officers at the city police department. We pick up in the midst of the direct examination of Cannon.

Q: Captain Cannon, as Desk Captain, what are your duties?

A: Well, I supervise the desk officers who receive calls and write up crime reports.

Q: Is there a standard procedure for filing crime reports?

A: Yes, I set up the procedures myself.

Q: What are those procedures?

A: Well, the investigating officer is required to call the desk from the scene of the crime. He dictates his report over the phone. The desk officer will type up the report as it is given over the phone.

Q: Is this the procedure for bank robberies?

A: Yes.

Q: Do you recognize this sheet of paper which has been marked as Government's Exhibit 1 for identification?

A: Yes. This is a crime report written by officer Davis on April 1, 2003. I recognize his handwriting.

Q: Who is Officer Davis?

A: He is the senior desk officer.

Q: What does the Government's Exhibit 1 for identification refer to?

A: It says: 'First National Bank Robbery—Initial Crime Report.'

Q: Who telephoned the report in?

A: Officer Harry Callahan. He's been on the force for five years.

Q: Does Davis know Callahan?

A: Yes, they're cousins.

Q: I offer Government's Exhibit 1 for identification in evidence.

(Pause 1)

Q: What does Government's Exhibit 1 say?

A: It says: 'Officer Callahan called in at 10:30 A.M. He reports the following:

1. He notes that the inside of the bank is riddled with bullet holes.

(Pause 2)

2. Officer Callahan spoke with an eye witness who was mortally wounded during the robbery. The witness said that Jackie Carney shot him. Callahan warned the witness that he shouldn't talk because he was going to die, but the witness kept talking.

(Pause 3)

3. Officer Callahan reports that a bank teller has estimated that the robber took $17,000.

Vignette
89

Hearsay: Official Records—Fed. R. Evid. 803(8)

Plaintiff Pomeroy is suing Defendant Mutual Insurance for failure to pay on a fire insurance policy when Plaintiff's store was destroyed by fire. The defendant calls a police officer to the stand.

Q: What is your name and occupation?

A: Robert Daley. I'm a City police officer.

Q: Directing your attention to the evening of February 1, 2004, were you on duty that night?

A: Yes and I responded to a call about a fire at the plaintiff's store.

Q: When did you arrive at the scene?

A: About 11 P.M.

Q: What did you see?

A: The store was burning out of control.

Q: Did you talk to anyone there?

A: Yes, I spoke to a firefighter.

Q: Did you make a report of that conversation?

A: Yes, I filled out an incident report that included his statement when I took a break about fifteen minutes later. I'm required to make and file a report as to all my investigations.

Q: Do you have the report with you?

A: Yes.

Q: Your Honor, I offer this report previously marked as Plaintiff's Exhibit 1 for identification in evidence as Plaintiff's Exhibit 1

Judge: *Admitted, if there's no objection.*

Q: Would you read the firefighter's statement in your report to the jury?

A: It says: "Firefighter James Smith said: 'I found three empty gasoline cans, some lighter fluid, and homemade torches near the point of origin of the fire. There is no question the fire was arson.' "

(Pause 1)

Q: As part of your investigation, did you talk to anyone else?

A: Yes, a bystander named Laura Wilson.

Q: Did you make a report of that conversation?

A: Yes, in the same report.

Q: Please read it to the jury.

(Pause 2)

A: 'Laura Wilson of 215 Elm Street said she was parked in her car across the street from the subject store just before the fire broke out and she saw a man running out of the store carrying a gasoline can.'

Vignette
90

Hearsay: Official Records—Fed. R. Evid. 803(8)

Plaintiff James Parsons sues Duffy Aircraft and the Secretary of the United States Navy for the wrongful death of his wife, Jane, a navy pilot, arising out of the crash of a Navy fighter plane during a training mission. Duffy Aircraft is the manufacturer of the fighter plane. Plaintiff alleges alternatively that the manufacturer defectively designed the aircraft and that the Navy improperly maintained the aircraft. At trial, Duffy Aircraft calls Emily Smith, a Navy captain and Judge Advocate General Officer, who was tasked to investigate the crash by the Navy. We pick up in the midst of her testimony.

Q: Captain, how did you come to investigate the crash of Lt. Parsons' aircraft?

A: The Judge Advocate General of the Navy ordered me to conduct an investigation of the crash pursuant to Navy regulations.

Q: Have you conducted investigations like this before?

A: Yes, on two other occasions. I am both a Navy pilot and a practicing attorney.

Q: Did you write a report of your findings?

A: I did.

Q: Showing you what's been marked at Defendant's Exhibit 1 for identification, please tell us what it is.

A: It's my report filed pursuant to the orders of my superiors regarding the crash of Lt. Parsons' aircraft.

Q: I offer Defendant's Exhibit 1 in evidence.

Objection. I object to the admission of the report because it is untrustworthy pursuant to Rule 803(8). If the report is admitted, I move to strike so much of the report as concludes that the cause of the crash was "pilot error."

(Pause 1)

Vignette
91

Hearsay within Hearsay—Fed. R. Evid. 805
Statements of Present Bodily Condition—Fed. R. Evid. 803(3)
Statements for the Purpose of Medical Diagnosis—Fed. R. Evid. 803(4)

Plaintiff George Grenard has sued Defendant Acme Paper Company for injuries he received when an Acme company truck struck Grenard's car after its driver allegedly ran a red light. The plaintiff was transported to Nita Memorial Hospital where he was treated in the emergency room and admitted for further treatment. Plaintiff called Grenard, who testified how the collision occurred and the nature of his injuries. The plaintiff then called Morgan Wright, the custodian of records at Nita Memorial Hospital. During the course of the direct examination, Ms. Wright testified as to how records are kept at the hospital, and identified Exhibit 7 as the ER records for the plaintiff on the date of the collision and his alleged injuries. We pick up in the midst of the direct examination of Ms. Wright.

Q: You honor, I offer Exhibit 7 in evidence.

Judge: It will be received.

Q: According to Exhibit 7, was a history taken from Mr. Grenard in the ER?

A: Yes.

Q: What was that history?

A: The record states in the history section: 'Patient complains of pain in his back and knees.' States that he 'was thrown forward and then backward when his car was hit by a large Acme Paper Company truck that collided with the left front-quarter panel of his car after running a red light.'

Move to strike.

(Pause 1)

Q: Does Exhibit 7 have a description of the physical exam of Mr. Grenard?

A: Yes, shall I read it?

Q: Yes, please.

A: 'Patient states that pain in his back has been increasing since the time of the collision. Lower back is tender to the touch. Patient cries out in pain when legs are raised above 45 degrees. Patient reports that he has no history of back problems . . . '

Motion to Strike.

(Pause 2)

Vignette
92

Hearsay: Former Testimony—Fed. R. Evid. 804(b)(1)

Defendant Joe Franklin and two codefendents were tried for armed robbery of a bank in June 2003. Despite claiming an alibi that they were out of the city on the day of the robbery, all three were found guilty. While the codefendants' convictions were affirmed on appeal, Franklin's was reversed and remanded for a new trial. The government is now retrying Franklin. The government's first witness is Robert Sprague, the court clerk at the first trial.

Q: What is your name and occupation?

A: Robert Sprague; I am assistant Clerk of Court for the U.S. District Court.

Q: Directing your attention to June 10, 2003, where were you?

A: I was serving as a clerk in the courtroom of Judge Jones in the trial of the defendant and two codefendants.

Q: Were you in court throughout the day?

A: I was present at the clerk's desk for every moment of the proceedings.

Q: Did Defendant Franklin's codefendant, Jackson, testify at the trial?

A: Yes, he did. He testified in his own defense.

Q: Did Franklin's lawyer cross-examine Jackson?

A: No, the judge asked him if he wanted to cross-examine, but he said no.

Q: Who was Franklin's lawyer at the first trial?

A: Joe Darrow, who died last year.

Q: When codefendant Jackson took the stand, what did he say?

(Pause 1)

Vignette
93

Hearsay: Former Testimony—Fed. R. Evid. 804(b)(1)
Hearsay: Statements Against Interest—Fed. R. Evid. 804(b)(3)
Hearsay: Impeaching the Hearsay Declarant—Fed. R. Evid. 806

Plaintiff Astral Stores brings an antitrust action against Defendant Newton Marketing claiming that Newton had been involved in price-fixing with another competitor, which has since been acquired by Newton in violation of the Sherman Act. Newton had earlier been prosecuted criminally by the Department of Justice, but the jury returned a verdict of "not guilty" in the criminal case. At trial of the civil action, Plaintiff calls Richard Jensen, a one-time official of Richards-Smythe, the former competitor, which has now been acquired by Newton.

Q: Mr. Jensen, did you know a man by the name of Gerald Erskine?

A: Yes, he was the President and CEO of Richards-Smythe. He died approximately one year ago.

Q: Did he testify in the Justice Department prosecution of Newton Marketing?

A: Yes, he testified for the government.

Q: Your honor, I now offer the transcript of Gerald Erskine's testimony in *United States v. Newton Marketing*.

Objection, hearsay. We would like to ask a few questions on voir dire.

Court: *Go ahead, but outside the hearing of the jury.*

Q: (By Defense Counsel):   *Did Mr. Erskine have an immunity agreement from the Government before he testified?*

A: *Yes, he did.*

Q: (By Defense Counsel):   *Your Honor, we object to any testimony of Mr. Erskine from the earlier trial on the grounds that the statements were not against Erskine's interest when made and because we cannot impeach him because he is dead. He has made similar statements consistent with his testimony at the earlier trial that we've discovered only since his death.*

(Pause 1)

Vignette
94

Hearsay: Statements Made Under Belief of Impending Death—Fed. R. Evid. 804(b)(2)

Bob Rutherford is on trial for reckless homicide. The prosecution alleges that because Rutherford drove his car in a reckless manner, he crashed into another car, killing three passengers and severely injuring a fourth. The prosecution also alleges that Rutherford was guilty of a hit-and-run offense because he immediately drove away after the accident. The investigating police officer was Bill Friday. The prosecution has called Officer Friday.

We pick up in the midst of Officer Friday's testimony.

Q: Officer Friday, when you first approached the victim's car, was anyone alive?

A: Yes, everyone was alive, but they were all severely injured.

Q: Did anyone survive?

A: Yes. Though three people died within two hours of the accident, one survived.

Q: Did the driver die?

A: Yes, he did.

Q: Did you speak with the driver before he died?

A: Yes.

Q: What did he say?

A: Well, he asked me how badly he was hurt. I told him as nicely as I could that it looked bad and he might die.

Q: Did he say anything more?

A: He said that if he lived through this, he would kill Bob Rutherford, because Rutherford caused the accident.

(Pause 1)

Q: Did you talk with anyone else?

A: Yes, I talked to the passenger in the front seat.

Q: Did he eventually die?

A: No, he's the one who survived.

Q: What was your conversation with him?

A: Well, I told him that he was badly injured and that he was probably wasn't going to make it. He nodded his head up and down.

Q: Was there anything else said?

A: Well, I asked him if he knew who drove the other car. He said that Bob Rutherford did it.

Q: How did he know it was Rutherford?

A: He said that he knew it was Rutherford because Rutherford is the only guy in town that drives as fast as the car that hit their car.

(Pause 2)

Q: Did you talk with anyone else?

A: Yes, with Jane Simmons. She also died.

Q: What was that conversation?

A: I told her, 'It looks bad, you're probably going to die.' I then asked, 'Was it Rutherford who hit you in his car?' She said, 'Yes,' closed her eyes, and died.

(Pause 3)

Vignette
95

Hearsay: Forfeiture by Wrongdoing—Fed. R. Evid. 804(b)(6)

Richard Carlson is being tried on charges of distribution of illegal drugs. Jack Johnson, a co-conspirator who was arrested with Carlson, has now been granted immunity in exchange for his testimony both before the grand jury and trial. Johnson's grand jury testimony provided the basis for indictment and Johnson is the government's first witness at trial.

Q: Mr. Johnson, do you know the defendant, Richard Carlson?

A: I have nothing to say.

Q: Mr. Johnson, I ask you again, do you know Richard Carlson?

A: I'm not testifying.

Judge: *Mr. Johnson, you have been granted immunity. No harm can come to you if you testify truthfully. I order you to answer the government's questions or be held in contempt.*

A: Do anything you like, Judge, but Carlson threatened my kids and I'd rather go to jail than lose them.

Judge: *Mr. Johnson, you are in contempt of court.*

A: I'm still not talking.

Q: Your honor, given this turn of events, the government would now offer an authenticated copy of Mr. Johnson's grand jury testimony in evidence.

Objection. Hearsay.

Vignette
96

Judicial Notice: Former Testimony—Fed. R. Evid. 201, 804(b)(1)

The plaintiff in a police misconduct case has sued two police officers and the Nita City Municipal Government, which employs them for a civil rights violation. Prior to trial, the plaintiff took the deposition of a third police officer who was present during the events that gave rise to the lawsuit. The deposition was taken in California where the former Nita City officer still resides. At the trial of the matter, the following occurs.

Q: What is your name?

A: Jane Doe.

Q: What do you do for a living?

A: I am a court reporter.

Q: Did you record and transcribe the deposition of Officer Debra Smith in this case?

A: Yes, in Modesto, California

Q: Showing you Plaintiff's 1 for identification, what is it?

A: The deposition of Officer Smith.

Q: Were the defendants represented at the deposition?

A: Yes.

Q: Your Honor, I ask you to take judicial notice that Modesto California is more than a hundred miles from this courthouse.

(Pause 1)

Q: Your Honor, I offer Plaintiff's Exhibit 1 in evidence and ask that I be allowed to publish Officer Smith's testimony to the jury.

(Pause 2)

Vignette
97

Impeaching the Hearsay Declarant—Fed. R. Evid. 806

In an automobile collision case, the plaintiff calls a police officer who was on traffic duty at the intersection where the collision occurred at the time of the collision. Plaintiff's counsel asks the following.

Q: Now Officer, directing your attention to twelve noon on August 1, 2003. Where were you?

A: At the intersection of Fourth and Main streets.

Q: Did you hear anything at that time?

A: Yes, I heard a crash of at least two automobiles.

Q: Did you hear anything else?

A: Yes, right after the crash, I heard a bystander shout, 'Oh my God, the Cadillac ran the light!'

Q: Did you later identify the bystander?

A: Yes, it was a man named Aloysius Monteith.

The examination and cross-examination of the witness was completed. After presenting the rest of its case in chief the plaintiff rested. During its case in chief, the defendant made the following offer to the court.

Q: *Your Honor, I offer as Defense Exhibit 1, a certified record of a perjury conviction for Aloysius Monteith that occurred by way of a guilty plea on November 12 of last year.*

Opponent: *Objection, counsel cannot impeach the credibility of a person who has never been a witness on direct examination.*

(Pause 1)

Vignette

98

Hearsay: Confrontation Clause

At the trial of Richard Toney for a January 15, 2003 bank robbery, the government has offered into evidence marked, stolen money linked to the bank robbery, money which was found on Toney at the time of his arrest. Toney has testified that he won the stolen money from Jimmy King while shooting dice a few hours after the time of the robbery.

On rebuttal, the government offered evidence from other witnesses who said they had been part of the dice game in question and it was Defendant Toney who had lost money to King.

Toney now calls John Smith, an FBI agent on surrebuttal.

Q: What is your name and occupation?

A: John Smith, I am a Special Agent with the FBI.

Q: Do you know a Jimmy King?

A: Yes.

Q: How do you know him?

A: I arrested him for the bank robbery involved in this case, but I later had him released for insufficient evidence.

Q: When you had him in custody, did he make any statements to you?

A: Yes.

Q: What did he say?

A: After giving him his *Miranda* warnings, he wanted to talk, and he said that he had been gambling with the defendant Toney late on the night of January 15, and that he, King, had lost $1,000 to Toney. He also said Toney started the game with very little money.

(Pause 1)

Vignette
99

Review Vignette One

The defendant, Jason Carson, is charged with larceny and extortion. The government claims that on or about January 29 of last year, the defendant stole a hundred pounds of uranium dioxide from the General Electric Company in Nita City and then extorted $10 million from the company for its return. The first witness for the government is Robert Anderson.

Q: State your name and address for the record.

A: Robert Anderson, 32 Stony Brook Road, Nita City, Pa.

Q: You work for General Electric, don't you?

(Pause 1)

Objection, leading.

(How should the court rule and why?)

A: Yes.

Q: What is your position?

A: I'm the plant manager.

Q: Were you so employed on January 29 of last year?

A: Yes.

Q: What happened that day?

(Pause 2)

(State the best objection.)

A: I sat down at my desk and started to work on the annual report. I'd been working for about a half an hour when the intercom buzzed. My secretary said an envelope addressed to me had been found on the floor in the outer office. She said it was marked 'urgent.'

(Pause 3)

Move to strike the last two sentences.

(How should the court rule and why?)

Q: What did you do?

A: Well, I thought I'd better have a look at it, so I told her to bring it in. A few seconds later she came into my office with a fat, white envelope, legal size, which said 'Anderson' and 'urgent' on the outside.

(Pause 4)

Objection, hearsay.

(How should the court rule and why?)

Q: What did you do?

A: I opened it. Inside was a ten or twelve-page handwritten letter and a small vial containing uranium dioxide.

(Pause 5)

(What is the best ground(s) to move to strike the last part of the answer?)

Q: What happened next?

A: I read the letter.

Note: Assume you saw the letter during discovery. It contains a threat to take the other one hundred pounds of uranium the writer said he had actually stolen and mail it to the President and every senator and congress person—unless the company paid the writer $10 million. It is the only alleged communication between the defendant and the company.

Q: What did it say?

(Pause 6)

(State all of the grounds for objection.)

Q: Mr. Anderson, I show you what has been marked as Government's 1 for identification and ask you to take a good look at it. Do you recognize it?

A: Absolutely. This is the letter I was just talking about.

Q: Could you be mistaken?

Q: Do you know Jason Carson, the defendant?

A: Yes, this letter was written in his handwriting.

Q: Your Honor, the Government offers number 1 as a full exhibit.

Objection, hearsay and lack of foundation.

(Pause 7)

(How should the court rule and why?)

Q: After you read the letter, what did you do?

A: I had my secretary put a call through to Charlene Rolland, our chief of security.

Q: Then what happened?

A: I told her what the letter said and she said, 'I'd be worried about this, Boss. This looks like a real threat. I'll check into it.'

(Pause 8)

Move to strike the answer as hearsay.

(How should the court rule and why?)

Q: Did you hear from her later?

A: She called and said that the letter appeared to be serious in that a hundred pounds of uranium dioxide were missing.

(Pause 9)

Q: That's all the questions I have. Thank you for coming to give your testimony, Mr. Anderson.

Court: *Any questions?*

Attorney: *Yes, your Honor.*

Q: You saw the CBS *Evening News* the night of January 29 of last year, didn't you?

A: Why, yes, I did.

Q: Dan Rather reported this story, didn't he?

A: Yes, he did.

Q: And didn't he say, and I quote, 'It may well be that the man charged with this crime has done this country a big favor by exposing the lax security at plants which manufacture nuclear materials.'

((Pause 10)

(State the two best objections.)

Q: By the way, Mr. Anderson, aren't you the same Robert Anderson who, on April 12, eight years ago, was convicted of the felony of assaulting a federal officer in this very court and before this very judge, for which you received two years probation?

(Pause 11)

Objection, improper impeachment.

(What is the correct ruling?)

A: You know, I was in a car accident three years ago and I can't remember anything that happened before that time, but I'm sure I wouldn't have done anything like that.

Q: Your Honor, I now offer a certified copy of the witness' conviction for assaulting a federal officer.

(Pause 12)

Objection, Your Honor, extrinsic evidence is inadmissible to impeach. What is the correct ruling and why?

Defense: *We have no further questions of this witness.*

Government: *Just a few questions on redirect, Your Honor.*

Court: *You may proceed.*

Q: Did you ever make arrangements to pay the money?

(Pause 13)

(State the best objection.)

A: Yes, with Agent Greenbaum of the FBI.

Q: No further questions of this witness.

Court: Very well. You may step down.

Court: *We call Richard Greenbaum.*

Q: Tell us about your occupation.

A: I am an FBI agent in Nita City, Nita. My actual title is Special Agent in Charge.

Q: Tell me about your training.

(Pause 14)

A: Well, I got a J.D. from Nita Law School in fifteen years ago and took a job with the Nita Police Department as a police legal advisor. The work wasn't very challenging, so I applied to join the FBI in two years later. They accepted me and I attended their six-month training course in Quantico, Virginia. The course covered all aspects of investigative work, including self-defense and weapons training. I worked at a number of offices until four years ago when I received my current assignment.

Q: Calling your attention to 10 A.M. on January 29 of last year, tell the members of the jury what happened.

A: I was in my office when I received a phone call from Charlene Rolland out at the General Electric plant. She's the Manager of Security there. She told me I'd better get out there right away and that they had a problem she didn't want to discuss over the phone.

(Pause 15)

Objection, lack of foundation

(How should the court rule and why?)

Objection, hearsay.

(Pause 16)

(How should the court rule and why?)

Q: What did you do?

A: I got there as fast as I could and took with me two other special agents, Cagey and Lockey.

Q: What happened?

A: Rolland showed me the note and I called FBI headquarters as I'm required to do whenever nuclear material has been stolen. I took the letter and also got a statement from Mr. Anderson and his secretary.

Q: Then what happened?

A: We had a tap put on the phone and waited for some contact from the extortionist who had stated in the letter he would be back in touch to arrange an exchange of the uranium for the money. The company got the money from the local bank.

Q: Did you get a call?

A: At about 1:27 P.M. that day, the defendant called.

(Pause 17)

(State the best objection.)

Q: What did he say?

(Pause 18)

Objection, hearsay.

(What should the proper ruling be and why?)

A: He said he would exchange the money for a map showing the location of the uranium. He demanded the exchange take place in parking lot of the Nita Train Station at 2:30 P.M that day.

Q: What did you do?

A: We went to the train station parking lot and set up our strike force which consisted of all available FBI special agents, state troopers, and the Nita Police Department's SWAT team.

Q: And then?

A: Promptly at 2:30 P.M., Anderson was standing in the parking lot with a briefcase in his hands. In the case was $10 million in used bills. We had made a list of the serial numbers of each of the bills.

Q: Did anyone arrive?

A: Yes, at about 2:45 P.M. a short man with a beard, wearing a tan trench coat, walked over to Mr. Anderson.

Q: About how far were you from where the defendant and Mr. Anderson were standing?

(Pause 19)

A: I'm not good with distances. It was a little less than the distance from home plate to first base on a professional baseball field.

Q: Your Honor, I ask that the court take judicial notice of the fact that the distance between home and first is 90 feet.

(Pause 20)

Objection, improper lay opinion and this is an improper item for judicial notice.

(How should the court rule and why?)

Q: What happened then?

A: Mr. Anderson handed the defendant the briefcase and the defendant gave Anderson a piece of paper. At that point, I had all units move in. The defendant didn't put up a fight.

Q: Looking around the courtroom, is the man who you saw talking to Mr. Anderson and later take the briefcase from him here today?

A: Yes, that's him over there.

Q: Let the record reflect the witness has identified the defendant.

Court: *Hearing no objection, the record will so reflect.*

Q: What did you do next?

A: We gave the defendant his *Miranda* rights. He said he wanted to talk to his lawyer so we asked him no questions. There were directions on the piece of paper. We followed them and recovered the missing uranium dioxide.

Q: What were the serial numbers of the bills in the briefcase Mr. Anderson carried?

A: I really can't remember all of them. They're in my report that I have here—would you like me to read them to you?

Q: Go ahead.

(Pause 21)

(State the best ground for the objection.)

Government: *No further questions.*

Defense Attorney: *We have a few questions on cross, Your Honor.*

Court: *Proceed.*

Q: Isn't it true that you previously described the man you saw in the field with Mr. Anderson as a tall man in a dark brown trench coat?

A: No.

Q: Doesn't your report filed with the FBI in the case say, and I quote, 'The man was tall and wearing a dark brown trench coat.'

(Pause 22)

Objection, hearsay.

(How should the court rule and why?)

A: Yes it does, but that's an error in the report.

Vignette
100
Review Vignette Two

MICHAELS	:	SUPERIOR COURT NITA COUNTY
	:	
V.	:	
	:	
MICHAELS	:	OCTOBER 30, 2003

TRANSCRIPT OF THE PROCEEDINGS AT TRIAL

Clerk: *Oyez, oyez, oyez. The civil term of the Superior Court is now open and in session. All persons having cause before this court draw nigh and give your attention according to law. The Honorable Voltaire Perkins presiding. Good morning, your Honor.*

Court: *Good morning. The first case on the trial docket, Mr. Clerk, appears to be the matter of* Michaels v. Michaels.

Clerk: *That's correct, your Honor. Susan Michaels, Plaintiff is suing her husband, John Michaels, on the grounds of mental cruelty. Mr. Michaels has cross-filed on the grounds of abandonment.*

Court: *Are both parties ready?*

Both Attys.: *Yes, your Honor..*

Court: *Very well, Mr. Clerk, swear everyone who is going to testify.*

Clerk: *Will all witnesses who are going to testify in this matter please rise and raise your right hand. Do you all swear that the testimony you are about to give in this matter is the truth, the whole truth and nothing but the truth, so help you God?*

Witnesses: *I do (in unison).*

Court: *Alright, let's proceed with an opening statement for the plaintiff.*

Plaintiff's Atty: *May it please the court. Members of the jury. As counsel for the plaintiff, Susan Michaels, it is my responsibility to briefly outline her position in this matter. Through a number of witnesses including Susan Michaels, Dr. Horace Johnson, and prominent members of this community, we will show that the defendant, Mr. John Michaels, inflicted great and unnecessary abuse upon his wife.*

The actions of the defendant, extending over a significant period of time, drove Susan Michaels to the brink of a complete emotional collapse and rendered her incapable of tending to the needs of her three young children. By publicly insulting her as a wife and mother, by privately accusing her of infidelity without cause, and by neglecting his marital duties, Mr. Michaels has made it clear that he has no intention of meeting his responsibilities as husband and father.

Despite her persistent efforts to reconcile their differences, Mr. Michaels and his representative have failed to reach a negotiated accord.

We are confident that you will accept the facts as presented by Susan Michaels and render judgment on her behalf. Thank you.

Court: *You may call your first witness, counsel.*

Q: Very well, your Honor. The plaintiff calls Reginald Hall. Mr. Hall, will you please state your name for the record?

A: Reginald W. Hall.

Q: Where do you live, Mr. Hall?

A: 115 Willow Haven Road.

Q: And you are Vice-President of Continental Construction Company and have been so employed for about ten years, is that right?

Objection, leading.

(Pause 1)

(How should the court rule and why?)

A: That's correct.

Q: And you are acquainted with Susan Michaels and with her husband, John Michaels?

(Pause 2)

A: Yes, I've known Susan most of her life. As for John, I've only known him for approximately eight years, but he's not very friendly, so I don't know him very well.

(Pause 3)

(*By opposing counsel*) *Objection, move to strike everything after 'eight years' is non-responsive.*

(How should the court rule and why?)

Q: Mr. Hall, have you been to visit Ed at the Michaels' home in Longmeadow that was purchased for them by Susan's father?

(Pause 4)

(State the best objection.)

A: Oh yes, on a number of occasions.

Q: Have you visited there recently?

A: Yes, I have.

Q: What happened during one of your recent visits to the Michaels' home?

(Pause 5)

(State the best objection.)

A: I can remember being invited over to Susan's for a dinner party along with a number of friends from the Club. As usual, Susan had prepared a lovely meal and was being a charming and gracious hostess. She takes such good care of her home and family, you know. In any event, we had delayed dinner in hopes that John would arrive. Just as we had about given up, John stormed in from God-knows-where, looking like a wild man, shouting at Susan in vile language and then he slammed the door and went out.

Move to strike the answer as improper opinion.

(Pause 6)

(What part, if any, should be stricken?)

Q: What did you and the other guests think about this incident?

(Pause 7)

(State the best objection.)

A: Well, naturally we were embarrassed for poor Susan and sympathized with her predicament.

Q: What did Mrs. Michaels do at that point?

A: Although mortified and quite upset, she struggled on. I remember her saying, 'I don't know what I'm going to do. He's always doing things like that. It's so embarrassing.'

(Pause 8)

Objection, hearsay.

(How should the court rule and why?)

Q: So it's your testimony that Mr. Michaels deliberately embarrassed his wife in public and caused her great mental distress?

(Pause 9)

(State the best objection.)

A: Yes, it is.

Q: Do you have information that such occurrences were commonplace in the public and private lives of the Michaels?

A: Yes, Susan complained to me on several occasions.

(Pause 10)

Objection, hearsay.

(How should the court rule?)

Q: Thank you, Mr. Hall. I have nothing further.

Cross-Examination of Reginald Hall

Q: Mr. Hall, you've known Mrs. Michaels for quite some time?

A: All of her life, twenty-eight or twenty-nine years, I guess.

Q: And you are a close friend of hers and of her family, isn't that so?

Objection, leading.

(Pause 11)

(How should the court rule and why?)

A: Yes, that's true.

Q: And it is also true that you are employed by Mrs. Michaels' father, J. Delbert Hathaway?

A: Yes, but . . .

Q: And this is the only position you have ever held since your graduation from college and it's your sole source of income, isn't it?

(Pause 12)

(State the best objection.)

A: Yes, but that has nothing to do with my testimony here.

(Pause 13)

(State the best objection.)

Q: However, it still remains that your employer is also the plaintiff's father?

A: Yes, I told you that.

Q: Now, turning to this 'incident' that you claim occurred at the Michaels' home. You know, don't you, that Professor Michaels was involved in a tenure decision at the university?

A: Well, I know now.

Q: At the time of this dinner party he was, wasn't he?

(Pause 14)

(State the best objection.)

A: I guess so.

Q: And when Professor Michaels came home that time he said, 'Susan, I didn't know you had guests. You know I must work on my research and can't stay. Why didn't you tell me?' Didn't he make that statement?

Objection, hearsay.

(Pause 15)

(How should the court rule and why?)

A: Well, he said something about working later.

Q: So, instead of cursing his wife as you stated on direct examination, all Professor Michaels did was to state that he had to work and couldn't stay for dinner, isn't that right?

(Pause 16)

Objection, asked and answered.

(How should the court rule and why?)

A: Well, his tone was clearly abusive and accusatory.

(Pause 17)

(State the best grounds to strike the answer.)

Q: Isn't it true, Mr. Hall, that you've recently been divorced by your wife of twelve years?

A: I'll connect this up in a few questions, your Honor.

Q: And isn't it true that one of the grounds for the divorce was the claim by your wife that you spent too much time at the club with Mrs. Michaels and others?

A: No, that's not true at all. She didn't like me going to the club.

Q: In any event, in addition to your devotion to Mrs. Michaels and her parents, it is also true that you've never liked Mr. Michaels, isn't it?

Objection.

(Pause 18)

(State the best ground of objection.)

A: I wouldn't say that.

Q: But you do believe that he doesn't fit in with your social group at the Club?

A: Well, he's not very athletic and he is a bit more academic than our crowd, but that doesn't mean I don't like him. As I said, he's not very friendly so I don't really know him.

Move to strike.

(Pause 19)

(How should the court rule and why?)

Q: I have nothing further of this witness.

Court: *You may call your next witness.*

Q: The Plaintiff calls Dr. Horace Johnson. Would you please state your name and business address?

A: Horace B. Johnson and my office is in Suite 1500, Medical Arts Building, Hospital Drive.

Q: What is your profession?

A: I am a physician, specializing in the practice of psychiatry.

Q: Have you come to court today prepared to state an opinion as to Mrs. Michaels' mental condition?

A: Yes.

Q: Let's talk about your qualifications to come to such an opinion, Dr. Johnson. Are you licensed to practice medicine in the state?

A: Yes.

Q: When were you licensed?

A: Fifteen years ago.

Q: Of what medical school are you a graduate?

A: Duke University Medical School.

Q: And where did you intern following medical school?

A: At Temple University Hospital in Philadelphia.

Q   Following your internship, did you undertake a residency?

A: Yes, I did.

Q: Doctor, is a residency a course of study and practical experience for a period of years under the supervision of specialists in a specific field?

A: Yes.

Q: And you specialized in psychiatry?

A: That's correct.

Q: Where and for how long did you serve your residency?

A: At Duke University Hospital for three years.

Q: Doctor, what is the American Board of Psychiatry?

A: This is a national organization of psychiatrists who have passed comprehensive written and oral examinations in the field of psychiatry.

Q: Are all doctors who specialize in psychiatry members of the American Board of Psychiatry?

A: No.

Q: Are you certified by the American Board of Psychiatry, Dr. Johnson?

A: Yes, I am.

Q: What additional educational experience do you have, Doctor?

(Pause 20)

(State the best objection.)

A: Well, I spent a year at the University of Prague Medical School in advanced experimental work in psychoanalysis.

Q: Do you belong to any medical societies?

A: Yes, American Medical Association, the State Medical Association, and the County Medical Society.

Q: Are you on the staff of any hospital?

A: Yes I am.

Q: Which hospital is that?

A: I am on the staff of the Nita University Hospital and associate director of the psychiatry department.

Q: Your Honor, I move that Dr. Johnson be declared an expert witness in the field of psychiatry.

Court: *Any objection?*

No, your Honor.

Court: *Dr. Johnson may be qualified as an expert in the field of psychiatry. You may proceed.*

Q: Thank you. Dr. Johnson, are you professionally acquainted with the plaintiff, Susan Michaels?

A: Yes, she is one of my patients.

Q: What was Mrs. Michaels' condition when she first came under your care in March, four years ago?

A: She was extremely depressed.

Q: Can you be more specific?

A: Not without my file and notes concerning her case.

Q: Dr. Johnson, I have here your notes from your first visit with Mrs. Michaels on March 21, 2001. Looking at them now, can you be more specific?

A: Yes, it says here that 'patient very depressed and at moderate-to-advanced stage of melancholy due to an apparent failure of her marriage.'

(Pause 21)

(State the best grounds of objection.)

Q: Did she give you a reason for this breakdown in her marriage?

A: Yes. She stated that her husband abused her, accusing her of infidelity and failure to care for their three children or their home. Also she said that he showed no interest in her, sexually or socially.

Objection, hearsay.

(Pause 22)

(How should the court rule and why?)

Q: Did you take any steps to assist Mrs. Michaels?

A: Yes, I did. We set up regular visitations for psychiatric counseling. I prescribed medications—a mild tranquilizer—and I attempted to get her husband to participate in joint counseling.

Q: What attempts did you make to get the cooperation of her husband?

A: Well, with Mrs. Michaels' permission and encouragement, I called him to see if we could arrange a conference. When I finally reached him he said that it was none of my business what he was doing, that he didn't need psychiatric help, and to confine myself to treating his wife.

(Pause 23)

Objection, hearsay.

(How should the court rule and why?)

Q: Didn't you tell Mr. Michaels the serious nature of her mental problems and possible complications if he ignored her request?

Objection, hearsay.

(Pause 24)

(How should the court rule and why?)

A: Yes, of course.

Q: So despite your warning, Mr. Michaels refused this attempt at reconciliation and counseling?

A: That's right.

Q: Dr. Johnson, are you aware that at some point Mrs. Michaels left her husband?

A: Yes, that was in the latter part of July 2001. She saw me before she left and I concurred in her judgment.

Objection, irrelevant.

(Pause 25)

(How should the court rule and why?)

Q: Why did you agree with the separation?

A: Because, despite my efforts, her mental condition had deteriorated, and in my opinion, the only chance she had to avoid a complete collapse was to dissolve the relationship with her husband.

Q: Doctor, it's your opinion, isn't it, that Mrs. Michaels' mental condition is related to her husband's attitudes and actions toward her?

(Pause 26)

(State the best objection.)

A: Yes, indeed. Her mental health was, and clearly is, affected by her husband's treatment of her.

Q: Doctor, do you have an opinion regarding whether or not the continuation of the marriage is conducive to the plaintiff's mental health?

(Pause 27)

Objection, improper ultimate opinion testimony.

(How should the court rule and why?)

A: Yes, I do.

Q: What is that opinion?

A: I believe that to continue the marriage will result in permanent mental harm to Mrs. Michaels.

Q: Thank you, Dr. Johnson. I have nothing further.

Cross-Examination of Dr. Horace Johnson

Def. Atty.: Dr. Johnson, you stated on direct examination that Mrs. Michaels' mental condition is related to mistreatment by her husband?

A: That is correct.

Q: Doctor, have you always been of that opinion?

A: Yes, I have.

Q: Directing your attention to the evening of Sunday, July 29, 2001, you were called to the Psychiatric Rehabilitation Center at University Hospital, weren't you?

A: Yes.

Q: At that time you treated the plaintiff, Susan Michaels, correct?

A: I saw her there. She couldn't reach me so she went to the hospital and they called me.

Q: Is it fair to say that she was in an extremely disturbed state at the time?

A: Well, I'm not sure I'd use those words. She was upset.

Q: Perhaps this will help you recall it better. I have here a standard University Hospital Psychiatric Evaluation form, signed by you and dated July 29, 2001, relating to Susan Hathaway Michaels. In this report you wrote, 'Susan very depressed. Claims that once again the children are too much for her and that if she can't get away from them, I'll go crazy. Have advised staying away from home until we can stabilize her condition. Have reached her parents to see if they can help since Susan unwilling to accept inpatient hospital care. Medication prescribed.'

Now, Doctor, in this report, you give an entirely different reason for Mrs. Michaels' departure from her home, don't you?

Objection, hearsay.

(Pause 28)

(How should the court rule and why?)

A: Well, it may appear that way, but that report doesn't . . .

Q: There's no need for explanations, Doctor. You know J. Delbert Hathaway, the plaintiff's father, don't you?

A: Just slightly. He is a member of the University Board of Trustees and is a city councilman. I've met him at various functions.

Q: Doctor, are you aware of the Continental Endowment Fund?

A: Yes. It awarded me and two of my colleagues a small grant last year to continue our research into the use of hypnosis as a psychological technique equally effective as many medications.

Q: The plaintiff's father is the principal contributor to the fund and sits on its board of directors, doesn't he?

A: Yes, I know that.

Q: And isn't it true, Dr. Johnson, that your grant is up for renewal within the next six months?

Objection, irrelevant.

(Pause 29)

(How should the court rule and why?)

A: Yes, but I'm not sure I know what you're driving at.

Q: Wasn't it your plan here today to attempt to protect Mr. Hathaway's daughter and thereby favorably influence his decision on your grant application?

Objection, irrelevant.

(Pause 30)

(How should the court rule and why?)

A: Certainly not! I resent your insinuation.

Q: Resent it or not, Doctor, it's a reasonable interpretation of the facts.

(Pause 31)

(State the best objection.)

Q: Now, have you continued to treat Mrs. Michaels since July 29, four years ago?

A: Yes, I have.

Q: In the course of treatment, has she mentioned to you anything about having an affair with another man?

Objection, irrelevant and inadmissible spousal privilege.

(Pause 32)

(How should the court rule and why?)

A: Well, she told me that since her husband has failed for many months to touch or sleep with her, she has been sexually deprived, and I agree with her.

Q: But she has told you that she has initiated a sexual relationship with another man, hasn't she?

Objection, irrelevant and prejudiced.

(Pause 33)

(How should the court rule and why?)

A: Not in so many words, but in substance that's true.

Q: So in reality, Doctor, the cause of this marital breakup is Mrs. Michaels' failure to care for her children and her illicit activity, not her husband's attitude toward her?

A: No, I wouldn't agree with that statement.

Q: I have no further questions at this time.